Australian-born Sharon Salloum learnt to cook authentic Syrian food from her mother and aunts. With an instinct for hospitality but no formal training, Sharon taught herself to run a commercial kitchen, and in 2007 she and her sister Carol opened their successful Almond Bar restaurant in Darlinghurst, New South Wales. Sharon is an active member of Sydney's food community and is passionate about the artistry of Middle Eastern food, participating in food tours and television series such as Food Safari on SBS. *Almond Bar* is her first cookbook.

To the person whose potential was always undervalued, Violet Salloum,
and to the person who always saw the potential in me, Carol Salloum

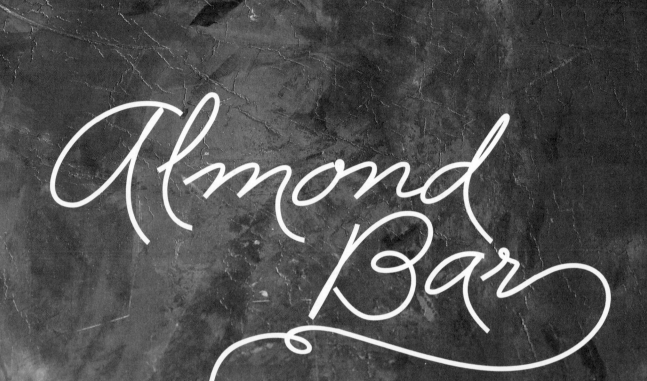

Almond Bar

SHARON SALLOUM

With photography by

ROB PALMER

jacqui
small

INTRODUCTION

I hope this book will show cooks of all types that Middle Eastern cuisine is one of beauty and enchantment. There are no fancy cuts, styles or machinery. But you do need to use the best and freshest ingredients. I like to think of it as 'food of the earth'; after all, its existence does date back to ancient Egypt. To this day, my family and relatives go no further than their gardens to source many of the fresh ingredients used in daily meals. What's a Middle Eastern garden without a bed of parsley and a bunch of fresh mint?

While there are certain staples of Middle Eastern cuisine, with many recipes there are variations between countries and sometimes even between different regions in the same country. Most of the recipes in this book are as I learnt them in a traditional Syrian household. Where possible I have included some background to each dish – the origins of many of them are scattered throughout the Middle East.

Now is a wonderful time to be a Syrian chef in Sydney. Interest in Middle Eastern food has really taken off in the past few years, and it is such a joy to see it finally starting to be better recognised and appreciated.

Who would ever have thought that the chickpea tree in my parents' garden would be the envy of produce suppliers all over the country? Or that there would be a widespread fascination with labne, a spread my mother would put on my school lunch wraps with home-cured olives? It is fantastic that Middle Eastern cuisine is now so accessible and celebrated. As a cook who has grown up observing society's changing attitude to Middle Eastern food, it has been an exciting journey for me. Along the way I have created new dishes, combining the old (traditional ingredients) and the new (modern techniques). These dishes, while categorically Middle Eastern, are uniquely my own.

However, I did get a little help to start the journey . . .

My mother's memories of her birthplace are complex – an infusion of sweet frustrations. She was the oldest of nine children, and her schooling finished at nine, when she began working as a cleaner to help support the family. Soon after, she became the primary carer for her grandparents, as her own mother had all the other children to care for.

My mother's only escape was cooking. She poured all her young dreams into her passion for food; her time in the kitchen was the only time she could call her own. In typical Syrian tradition, she would sometimes cook for every man and his donkey, as relatives and neighbours were always dropping in for dinner. Cooking became my mother's refuge, and her refuge was a blessing for anybody fortunate enough to taste her food.

Throughout her adult life my mother has maintained her passion for cooking and stayed true to her origins. At times she would veer away from the culinary practices passed down to her from her mother, but she never forgot them. As a child, I used to wonder why she devoted so much time and energy to sourcing, preparing and cooking food. Whenever I asked her, she'd always answer in a rush, 'One day you'll understand', as she prepared the myriad of dishes for dinner that night, as if all life on earth depended on feeding her family each day – and for her it did. I understand now.

I still love watching my mother cook. I often take little videos to keep of her putting dishes together, picking herbs in the garden, pouring stocks into different pots. As a child, I used to drive her crazy with questions about methods and cooking times and flavours and possible substitute ingredients. Nothing has changed! Except that now I tower over my mother and get in the way more than I did back then.

My father believes that food fixes everything. In our home, when you're not feeling well, it's because you don't eat enough. Or if someone is in a bad mood, they're not eating enough. 'Why are you tired? You just do not eat enough.' So it is understandable that an appreciation of food was passed down to my brothers, my sister and me from a young age.

Clockwise from bottom left: *my brother Steven, his wife Tatiana, my cousin Rima, Uncle Tony, Dad, my sister Carol, Aunty Azizi, Aunty Adele, Mum and me*

According to Syrian tradition, sharing meals is an essential part of spending time with family and friends – you should never eat alone. This belief is underpinned by a subtle culinary rivalry between the women in a family, fuelled by inspection and comparison, in the constant quest for perfection and the prized title of 'best cook in the family'. Our family gatherings were always preceded by a week-long marathon of preparation, which involved sourcing, cleaning, marinating, chopping, mixing, smoking and baking all sorts of food. The aim was to please everyone – to create food so scrumptious that even the harshest critic would succumb. I was fascinated by the whole drama of it, and would mentally take notes of everybody's methods, and also their critiques of everybody else. Little did I realise as a child that such information would become so invaluable down the track; at the time, I just thought it was all good fun!

Apart from this rivalry and having to swear to every aunty (out of earshot of the next) that her tabouli was the best – after my mother's, of course – these gatherings provided one of my greatest learning platforms. I would enquire into and be entrusted with the secret techniques of different family members, and these have helped to shape my own cooking style to this day. Today, the women in my family often come to me for hints and advice; as silly as it may sound, these are some of my proudest moments.

When my sister Carol came up with the idea of opening our restaurant Almond Bar, to bring to life my mother's love of food, I couldn't resist. Initially, my fears about not being able to emulate the passion my mother puts into her food were overwhelming, but I soon learnt that it's okay to make mistakes along the way, and that often these are blessings in disguise because you end up creating something even better. Just as we both believed in the beauty of my mother's creations, my sister believed I would be the one to deliver them to our customers. After much blood, sweat and tears, I would like to believe that I have done my parents and family proud.

The other reason for creating Almond Bar was to share the Middle Eastern service and hospitality that Carol and I had grown up with. There was a reason I loved the buzz of family gatherings; the search for reassurance, the big banquets, the comparing of notes, the belief that less was never more. It was because the importance of celebrating food, of sharing and hospitality, were instilled in us from an early age. I remember serving cups of tea and coffee, sweets (candies) and biscuits (cookies) from when I was as young as eight years old. My sister Carol was even younger when she made her first stovetop-brewed pot of coffee! We were brought up by parents who were constantly entertaining relatives and friends. We could all be yelling at each other, but as soon as there was a knock on the door, we were all showcasing our best smiles.

Every dish on the Almond Bar menu has been through an often-conflicting 'panel' review process: it has to appeal to my sister's palate, circumvent my mother's suspicion of anything that is not traditional, and meet my cousin Rima's demands that I create something new.

I love being part of the next generation of Middle Eastern cooks. My aim is to recreate, and improve if possible, the food we have loved and shared over the years, to give it the respect it deserves and to show an appreciation for every dish. That respect and appreciation has been instilled in me by my mother, first and foremost, but also by the other women in my family. I consider everything I have been taught to be sacred, and I am humbled to have had such great teachers and mentors. By way of thanks, I can only hope to continue to shed light on Middle Eastern cuisine and help stir greater appreciation for this ancient cuisine and its heritage.

I'm thankful that my passion for cooking comes from my mother, and not from that place of solitude and sacrifice from which her own flourished. This book is an ode to success born of struggle and to where it all began, in my mother's heart. ◆

Clockwise from top left: *Me cooking lamb skewers; Dad and Carol; Aunty Adele, Mum and me enjoying the meal; Mum smoking aubergine (eggplant) for baba ghanouj*

BALADIEH CHEESE

Baladieh (meaning 'country') is a semi-soft white cheese made from cow's milk. It is usually stored in its brine, but can also be purchased in vacuum-sealed packs (less salty than the cheese in brine). If you can't find it, the next-best thing would be feta.

BASTURMA

Also known as Armenian air-dried beef, this cured meat is coated in a blend of dried herbs, garlic and spices, which varies according to the origin of its creator. It should not be confused with pastrami, which is cured and smoked.

BROAD (FAVA) BEANS

Called 'foul' (pronounced 'fool') in the Middle East, broad (fava) beans are commonly used in stews or sautéed with other greens. Available fresh, dried or canned in brine, the canned version is perhaps best known as the star ingredient in the traditional breakfast dish 'foul medammas' (see page 69).

BURGHUL (BULGUR WHEAT)

Burghul (bulgur wheat) is cracked wheat and is made mostly from durum wheat; it is prepared by parboiling the wheat grain, drying it and then removing the outer layer of bran. It comes in several varieties, including brown and white grains or powdered, fine and coarse. Each variety is suited to a particular use. Coarse burghul (bulgur wheat) is best in soups or pilafs; fine is commonly used in kibbeh dishes and tabouli or other salads; and powdered burghul (bulgur wheat) tends to be added to flours or semolina in desserts.

CASSIA BARK

Cassia is a member of the same family as cinnamon, but has a flavour that is less delicate and a little sweeter. In Syrian cooking, dried cassia bark is used instead of cinnamon sticks to flavour teas, stocks, stews and sauces. Cinnamon can be used if necessary, but cassia will give a more authentic flavour.

CHICKPEAS

Known as 'hummus' in Arabic, there's a lot more to this mighty legume than meets the eye. Buying good chickpeas is an extremely important exercise in Middle Eastern cooking and can be the crucial difference between good falafel and great falafel; good hummus and great hummus. Take the time to pick out any dark chickpeas or scraps of dirt before you soak them overnight.

FREEKEH

High in protein, freekeh is made by harvesting wheat while its grains are green. Traditionally the whole grains are sundried and then flame-grilled to give them a subtle smoky flavour. The wheat is then rubbed together ('frekeh' – to rub together) to create what looks like coarse green burghul (bulgur wheat). This wonderful grain is used in much the same way as coarse burghul (bulgur wheat) in pilafs and as a replacement for rice.

GREY COURGETTE (ZUCCHINI)

The grey courgette (zucchini) or 'kousa', is a member of the squash family. It has a lovely light flavour, slightly firmer flesh than regular green courgette (zucchini), and takes a little longer to cook. This combination makes it the perfect vegetable for stuffing with rice, vegetables and meats and leaving to roast slowly and gently. The result is tender flesh that holds together, but can be sliced through like room-temperature butter.

HALOUMI

People are often surprised to learn that in Middle Eastern households haloumi is generally eaten fresh, not cooked. Fresh haloumi is a stretched-curd cheese, created in a similar way to mozzarella. Like mozzarella, it was originally made with buffalo milk, but these days it is more likely to be cow's milk. Fresh haloumi is usually flavoured with mint and can be purchased in vacuum-sealed packs or in jars of brine.

KATAIFI PASTRY

Commonly described as 'shredded pastry', kataifi is made by pouring the pastry batter through a fine mesh onto a metal hot plate. It is mostly used in dessert recipes, but also works really well in savoury dishes, such as pastry-wrapped prawns (shrimp) or chicken. For the best flavour and texture, this pastry should be baked or fried.

KISHK POWDER

This amazing ingredient is created by combining yoghurt and burghul (bulgur wheat) and leaving them to ferment for a period of time. It is then dried completely (traditionally in the sun) until it can be rubbed between the hands to form a fine powder. Kishk has a mildly sour flavour and is normally used to thicken soups and stews.

LAMB

Lamb is a highly regarded meat in Middle Eastern cooking. It is enjoyed both raw and cooked, on skewers and pizzas, and in soups, stews and pastries. As with any meat, different cuts are used for different purposes, but the cut I grew up with (and continue to use in the restaurant) is the 'eye' meat from a boned loin of lamb, which is thickly cut into noisettes. These are similar to pork escalopes and are the leanest lamb cut. They simply melt in your mouth. If you can't get your hands on 'eye' meat, backstrap makes a good substitute. This beautiful cut comes from the loin or mid-section of the lamb and can also be cooked just about any way, while retaining a lovely texture and flavour.

MIDDLE EASTERN BREAD

Also known as Lebanese or flat bread, Middle Eastern bread is an integral part of any Syrian meal. Often served fresh, it is also delicious fried. To do this, cut each piece of bread into eight triangles. Deep-fry in small batches in light olive oil until lightly browned on both sides (this should take a minute or so). Remove with tongs and drain on kitchen paper (paper towels), then allow to cool before serving.

MOGHRABIEH

Often labelled as 'giant couscous' or 'Israeli couscous', this semolina-based grain is like regular couscous, only significantly larger. It has a similar texture and flavour to pasta, so it takes on any sauce or accompaniment very well.

ORANGE BLOSSOM JAM

Orange blossoms are the flowers of the orange tree. The delicate white petals are hand picked and are used to make orange blossom products such as jam and water (see below). The sticky jam is a beautiful red colour, and is normally used as a final flourish on top of Middle Eastern desserts.

ORANGE BLOSSOM WATER

Orange blossom water is a clear, aromatic liquid made from distilled orange blossoms. Because of its strong scent and flavour it is best used sparingly so it doesn't overpower the other flavours in the dish. It is most commonly used in desserts, creams, fruit salads and jams, and to perfume sugar syrups that are poured over Middle Eastern sweets (candies); however, it can also be used in some savoury dishes to reduce the gamey flavour of certain meats and bring out their natural sweetness.

PICKLED TURNIPS

These gorgeous pink pickles ('leffet makboos') are simply made by combining sliced beetroot (beet) and a little garlic with the briny liquid used to pickle turnips. They can be served as an accompaniment to almost any savoury dish.

PIMENTO

The whole pimento or allspice is also known as Jamaican pepper, since it is commonly used to spice jerky. In Middle Eastern cooking, whole pimento is lightly crushed and added to soups, stews, stocks (broths) and marinades. Freshly ground pimento is also a key ingredient in Syrian mixed spice (see page 13). You can purchase ground allspice from any supermarket.

POMEGRANATE MOLASSES

This little gem seems to be popping up everywhere these days. Made from the slow-cooked flesh and juice of pomegranate seeds, this thick, syrupy condiment works really well in tomato-based dishes and stews, as an aid to tenderising slow-cooked roasted meats, or as a replacement for balsamic vinegar in just about anything. Just remember to use a light touch – a little goes a long way!

SEMOLINA

Made from durum wheat, this fine grain is generally used in Middle Eastern cooking to make sweet dishes, often in combination with other flours to create biscuits (cookies) and sweets (candies). Sometimes it is toasted before use to enhance its natural flavours.

SPLIT CHICKPEAS

Most people have heard of split peas, but are unfamiliar with split chickpeas. These are smaller than regular chickpeas and are split in half during the drying process. In Middle Eastern cooking they are mainly used in vegetarian dishes and make a perfect addition to stuffings due to their smaller size. Buy them dried and make sure you soak them overnight before use.

SUGAR SYRUP

Sugar syrup (or 'ater') is a key ingredient in Middle Eastern sweets (candies) and desserts, and is often served with the dish so that people can adjust the sweetness to suit individual tastes. You can buy it from Middle Eastern food stores but it's very easy to make your own. To do this, combine 220 g (1 cup) granulated sugar, ½ teaspoon lemon juice and about 100 ml (½ cup) water in a small saucepan and bring to the boil over high heat, stirring constantly until the sugar has dissolved. Add 1 teaspoon rosewater and stir for another 4–5 minutes. Remove from the heat and leave to cool completely, then chill for at least half an hour before using. The syrup will thicken during this time. This will make about 300 ml (1¼ cups), and the syrup can be stored in an airtight bottle or container in the fridge for up to a week. Omit the rosewater if you like, or replace it with orange blossom water or a combination of rosewater and orange blossom water.

SUJUK

The original makers of these fermented sausages were the Turkish and the Armenians. Due to the large number of Armenians living in Syria, the sausages have been readily absorbed into Armenian–Syrian cuisine, celebrating a wonderful array of spices. Ground beef is combined with garlic, sumac, cumin, salt, fenugreek, fennel and many other spices, stuffed into casings and left to dry for several weeks. The sausages are then sliced and used in dishes such as scrambled eggs, savoury pastries and pies.

SUMAC

The deep red-coloured sumac berry grows on a small shrub or tree. It is picked, dried and crushed to create ground sumac. Its light citrus flavour is an important ingredient in za'atar and fatoush salad, but sumac is also used in spinach pastries or sprinkled over dips such as labne or hummus. It also works well with seafood, and any other dish that calls for a subtle hint of lemon.

SWEET CHEESE

Originally, sweet cheese was made from buffalo milk but these days cow's milk is used. Like mozzarella, it is made by stretching and kneading a treated curd, giving a stretchy consistency when cooked. It is called 'sweet cheese' as no salt is added during its production. It is mostly used in sweets (candies) and desserts, such as halowet eil jiben (see page 188).

TAHINI

There seems to be an air of mystery around this beautiful ingredient (essentially crushed sesame seeds). There are two main types of tahini: unhulled tahini leaves the sesame husks intact, while hulled tahini is smoother, has a lighter colour and less bitter flavour, and is the one most commonly used. Black tahini is made from unhulled black sesame seeds, with additional health benefits due to increased levels of antioxidants. Its flavour is very similar to hulled 'white' tahini and it can be used in all the same ways. When buying tahini, don't just grab any old jar off the supermarket shelves. You're looking for a nice light cream colour, not too dark or too bright, and there should not be a thick layer of oil on top. If the packaging prevents you from seeing the tahini, ask your Middle Eastern food supplier for a recommendation.

WILD THYME

Just as people from the Middle East call both chickpeas and the famous chickpea dip 'hummus', we call both wild thyme and the well-known spice mix 'za'atar'. This is because these ingredients are the flavour base of their respective preparations. Wild thyme has a slightly stronger flavour than regular thyme, with longer leaves, but the two are reasonably interchangeable. To make za'atar spice mix (see page 12), wild thyme is picked and sundried, then ground. Wild thyme is also used fresh in salads and can be used in marinades for meats, fish and vegetables. ◆

MIDDLE EASTERN FOOD SUPPLIERS

UK

Arabica Food & Spice Company

The Arabica Food & Spice Company Ltd, Unit 257, Grosvenor Terrace, London, SE5 0NP
020 7708 5577
www.arabicafoodandspice.com
An online shop with a vast range of Eastern Mediterranean products from aromatics and flavourings, herbs and spices, to all types of sweets, pickles and pastes.

Bart

The Bart Ingredients Company Ltd, York Road, Bristol, BS3 4AD
0117 977 3474
www.bart-ingredients.co.uk
An online shop selling a wide range of dried herbs and spices and pastes. They can also be bought from certain supermarkets in the UK.

Bismillah Food Store

3 Nicolson Square, Nicolson Street, Edinburgh EH8 9BH
0131 662 4308
A convenience store selling halal meat and grocery food products from all around the world including the Middle East.

Damas Gate

81 Uxbridge Road, London W12 8NR
020 8743 5116
A great supermarket stocking lots of Middle Eastern groceries including falafels, fruit and vegetables and herbs and spices.

Green Valley

36–37 Upper Berkeley Street, London W1H 5QF
020 7402 7385
This grocery store stocks a wide range of Middle Eastern products including fresh baklava, fruit and vegetables, bread, spices, sweets, coffee and much more. A food lover's paradise.

Ottolenghi

287 Upper Street, London N1 2TZ
020 7288 1454
www.ottolenghi.co.uk
There are several branches of Ottolenghi throughout London but this is the largest. There is also a restaurant, which is open for breakfast, lunch and dinner, but reservations are advised for dinner. The shop stocks a wide range of Middle Eastern products ranging from dried fruit and nuts, syrups, spices including za'atar, grains including freekeh and mograbieh as well as pickles and preserves. There is also a mail order service.

Persepolis

28–30 Peckham High Street, SE15 5DT
020 7639 8007
www.foratasteofpersia.co.uk
This is the place to go for everything Middle Eastern. If you don't live in Peckham then visit the online shop where one can buy herbs, spices, bulgur wheat, and more.

Steenbergs

6 Halikeld Close, Baker Business Park, Melmerby, Ripon, HG4 5GZ
01765 640088
www.steenbergs.co.uk
An online shop specialising in organic and fairtrade herbs, spices and other dried grocery products from all over the world including the Middle East, such as za'atar, seven-spice powder and falafel mixes. This is definitely worth a look.

Taj Natural Foods

98–99 Western Road, Brighton, East Sussex BN1 2LA
01273 735728
This shop stocks a wide range of products from all over the world including the Middle East. They have a wide variety of fresh fruit and vegetables as well as haloumi and dried herbs and spices, lentils, beans and grains.

Tipaza Grocery Shop

143 Lisburn Road, Belfast BT9 7AG
028 9066 0808
A grocery store selling a wide range of Middle Eastern food including halal meat, semolina, cheese, pulses and orange blossom water to name but a few.

Yasar Halim

386–390 Green Lanes, London N4
020 8340 8090
495 Green Lanes, London N4 1AL
ww.yasarhalim.com
A wonderful Cypriot/Turkish supermarket selling everything from fresh fruit and vegetables to fresh breads and baklava. There are two shops in London one in Haringay and the other in Palmers Green.

US

Babylon Market

3954 E. Speedway Blvd, Tucson, AZ, 85712

(520) 232-3700

www.babylonmarkettuscon.com

A Middle Eastern market in Tuscon stocking foods from all over the world including the Middle East. They have a wide range of products such as pitta bread, fresh fruit and vegetables including dates, olives and Perisan cucumbers, tahini, feta, labne and yoghurts.

Buy Lebanese

+961 3 602405

www.buylebanese.com

This US nationwide online store specialises in Middle Eastern cuisine including breads, herbs and spices, pine nuts, burghul (bulgur wheat), and much more.

Dayna's Market

26300 Ford Road, Suite 239, Dearborn Heights, MI 48127

313-999-1980

www.daynasmarket.com

An online shop specialising in Middle Eastern and Mediterranean products including breads, herbs and spices, dried fruit, beans, olive oil, yoghurt, labne and tahini.

Hashems Nut and Coffee Gallery

13041 W Warren Ave, Dearborn, MI 48126

888-581-3212

www.hashems.com

A family-run business originally providing quality coffee, fresh roasted nuts and hand mixed spices available in store or online. There is now a huge range of Middle Eastern foods available from olive oil, dried fruit, breads, beans and peas, bulgur wheat, vermicelli, lentils, couscous and freekeh.

Middle East Food Market

4097 Peralta Blvd, Fremont, CA 94536

510-739-3800

www.mefoodmarket.com

This online store offers a wide variety of Mediterranean and Arabic products including cheeses, such as labne and haloumi, tahini, spices, halal meat products, candies and bakery items fresh to order.

Shamra.com

2650 University Blvd, Wheaton, MD 20902

(301) 942-9726

www.shamra.com

An online shop that specialises in Middle Eastern food and stocks a wide range of products including dried beans and peas, lentils, grape leaves, bulghur wheat, olives, different types of olive oil and much more.

Zamouri Spices

Zamouri Spices, an Elbertai Company LLC,

1250 N. Winchester Blvd. Suite I, Olathe, KS 66061

913-829-5988

www.zamourispices.com

This online shop specialises in hard-to-find spices from all over the world including the Middle East. They stock individual spices, spice blends and spices by the pound as well as orange blossom water and tahini. ◆

Za'atar

OREGANO & THYME SPICE BLEND

MAKES ABOUT 100 G (¾ CUP)

─────────────

2½ tablespoons dried wild thyme
(or regular thyme can also be used)

2½ tablespoons dried oregano

2 teaspoons salt flakes

2 tablespoons ground sumac

2 tablespoons roasted sesame seeds

─────────────

Za'atar is a slightly citrussy spice blend, dating back to ancient Egypt, used to add flavour and also as a dry rub or marinade. There are many different varieties; this is the one used most in Syria and Lebanon, and is a staple in our household. When we were growing up, it was often carried back from Syria in someone's luggage; there is nothing like Syrian sumac berries. This subtle spice blend is often eaten for breakfast as either a dipping spice or on a thin, homemade pizza base (see page 36).

Using a coffee or spice grinder, grind the wild thyme, oregano and salt together until medium fine. To avoid a powdery dust, run the mixture through a fine sieve, reserving the mix in the sieve, and discarding the powder that gets through. Stir in the sumac and sesame seeds.

Place in an airtight container or jar and store in a cupboard away from sunlight for up to 12 months.

Za'atar halabeh

ALEPPO ZA'ATAR

MAKES ABOUT 200 G (1½ CUPS)

─────────────

30 g (¼ cup) dried wild thyme
(or regular thyme can also be used)

2 tablespoons cumin seeds

2 tablespoons coriander seeds

1 star anise

2 tablespoons salt flakes

35 g (¼ cup) unsalted peanuts

25 g (¼ cup) ground sumac

35 g (¼ cup) roasted sesame seeds

─────────────

At good Middle Eastern grocers, you are sure to find at least five different varieties of za'atar to choose from, and people also make their own mix at home. In Beirut, the most prized za'atar includes delicate white thyme flowers; the result is a light-coloured za'atar rarely found in shops, but made by hand at home. In Aleppo they prefer to grind the sesame seeds, which gives the mixture a browner appearance. This recipe is for the Aleppo version, but my advice is to taste a few varieties and see which you prefer. You should be able to eat the za'atar dry with a spoon, and it should not be powdery or have bits of stem in it.

Using a coffee or spice grinder, grind the thyme, cumin and coriander seeds together until fine. To avoid a powdery dust, run the mixture through a fine sieve, reserving the mix in the sieve, and discarding the powder that gets through. Transfer to a bowl.

Grind the star anise and salt flakes until fine and add to the bowl. Grind the peanuts until medium–fine, then add to the bowl with the sumac and sesame seeds. Mix together well.

Place in an airtight container or jar and store in a cupboard away from sunlight for up to 12 months.

Sub-ah b'har
SEVEN-SPICE MIX

MAKES ABOUT 120 G (⅔ CUP)

─────────────────

2 tablespoons freshly ground black pepper

1 tablespoon sweet paprika

2 tablespoons ground cumin

1 tablespoon ground coriander

1 tablespoon ground cloves

1 teaspoon freshly grated nutmeg

1 teaspoon ground cinnamon

1 tablepoon ground allspice or pimento (optional)

─────────────────

Seven-spice mix is another staple in any Middle Eastern pantry. I have always known the mix as sub-ah b'har (seven spices), but, depending on who is putting it together, the seven spices might easily turn into nine or eleven. There are two ways to make it. The first is to crush whole pods or seeds in a coffee or spice grinder (this is the method my mother prefers). However, when you're pressed for time, a mix of ready-ground spices still gives a wonderful result.

Mix all the ground spices together until well combined.

Place in an airtight container or jar and store in a cupboard away from sunlight for up to 12 months.

Syrian b'harat
SYRIAN MIXED SPICE

MAKES ABOUT 100 G (JUST UNDER 1 CUP)

─────────────────

35 g (⅓ cup) ground allspice or pimento

25 g (¼ cup) ground cinnamon

25 g (¼ cup) freshly grated nutmeg

2 tablespoons ground cloves

─────────────────

Naturally, there is also a Syrian version of the seven-spice mix. Very easy to make, this one is probably a little more user-friendly than traditional seven-spice mix. The Syrian version is used mostly in Aleppo and Damascus.

Very simply, mix all the ingredients together in a bowl.

Place in an airtight container or jar and store in a cupboard away from sunlight for up to 12 months.

Sauces & dips

Baba ghanouj

SMOKED AUBERGINE DIP

MAKES ABOUT 450 G (JUST OVER 2 CUPS)

---

2 large aubergines (eggplants)

140 g (½ cup) tahini

60 ml (¼ cup) lemon juice

1 clove garlic, crushed

2 teaspoons salt flakes

ground sumac, finely diced tomato
and olive oil, to garnish

Middle Eastern bread, to serve

Baba ghanouj is known mainly as a dip, but it is much more than that on the Middle Eastern table. It is eaten with barbecued dishes such as lamb skewers and barbecued chicken, but it also goes well with just about any vegetarian dish or simply with a side of tabouli. The smokiness of the aubergine (eggplant) is a beautiful accompaniment to any meal.

Prick each aubergine (eggplant) with a fork in three places. Using tongs, turn the aubergines (eggplants) over an open flame until they are charred all over and the skin is starting to crack. The whole point is to burn the skin so don't worry when this happens. Place the charred aubergines (eggplants) in a bowl of cold water to cool for about 10 minutes, then hold them under running water and remove the stalks and peel off the blackened skin. Open the aubergines (eggplants) and remove as many seeds as possible from the centre. You may not be able to take out every last seed, just do your best as this will help rid the aubergine (eggplant) of any bitterness. Once cleaned, place the aubergine (eggplant) in a colander to drain.

Place the aubergines (eggplants), tahini, lemon juice, garlic and salt in a food processor and blend for 3–4 minutes or until well combined. The baba ghanouj should not be completely smooth – slightly lumpy is good, but you don't want any big chunks of aubergine (eggplant) in the mix. Scrape down the sides of the bowl and pulse a couple of times.

Spoon the baba ghanouj into a shallow bowl and garnish with a sprinkling of sumac, some finely diced tomato and a drizzle of olive oil. Serve with Middle Eastern bread.

Store in an airtight container in the fridge for up to 5 days.

Hummus aswed

BLACK TAHINI & CHICKPEA DIP

MAKES ABOUT 500 G (JUST UNDER 2 CUPS)

½ teaspoon bicarbonate of soda (baking soda)

200 g (1 cup) dried chickpeas

140 g (½ cup) black tahini

juice of 2 lemons

1 small clove garlic, crushed

½ teaspoon salt flakes, or to taste

extra virgin olive oil and sweet paprika,
to garnish (optional)

Middle Eastern bread, to serve

A good hummus is all about getting the right balance of ingredients, and the key to its success is to use large dried chickpeas, at least 9 or 10 mm (⅓ in). In Syria, there is much focus on the texture of the dip – so much so, that some restaurants will peel every cooked chickpea to achieve an amazingly creamy consistency. I don't recommend that though! For something a bit different, I have replaced the regular tahini with a black sesame-seed tahini, whose natural flavours enhance the beauty of this simple and widely loved dip. If you prefer traditional hummus, you can of course replace the black tahini with regular tahini.

Dissolve the bicarbonate of soda (baking soda) in a large bowl of water, add the chickpeas and soak overnight. Rinse and drain.

Bring a large saucepan of water to the boil, add the chickpeas and return to a simmer. Cook for about 40 minutes or until the chickpeas are tender and can be crushed between two fingers. Drain and allow to cool.

Place the cooled chickpeas in a food processor and blend until as smooth as possible. You may need to add a tablespoon of water to bring the chickpeas together if they start sticking to the side of the processor. Add the tahini, lemon juice, garlic and salt and blend until well combined.

At this point the dip will become quite thick and difficult to blend. Gradually add enough water to thin it out to a smooth paste – start with 2 tablespoons and take it from there. Don't add too much or it will turn into a sauce. Taste and add more salt if you think it needs it.

Transfer the hummus to a shallow bowl and finish with a drizzle of olive oil and a sprinkling of sweet paprika (if using). Serve with Middle Eastern bread.

Store in an airtight container in the fridge for up to 4 days.

Tarator

TAHINI SAUCE

MAKES ABOUT 375 ML (1½ CUPS)

_____

1 clove garlic, peeled and left whole,
plus extra if needed
100 g (generous ⅓ cup) tahini
½ teaspoon salt flakes
80 ml (⅓ cup) lemon juice, plus extra if needed

_____

This beautiful sauce is the traditional Arab accompaniment to falafel. It can be used as a sauce or marinade for potatoes, as well as with fish and chicken dishes. When I was growing up, Mum would make tarator with chopped parsley mixed through and serve it with fried fish. When I first came across tartare sauce at a fish and chips shop as a child, I was disappointed that it had a mayonnaise base, and glad that we didn't have to buy it because Mum knew how to make it the right way.

Process the garlic in a small food processor until finely chopped. Add the tahini and blend until combined, then add the salt and lemon juice. If the tarator seems a bit thick, add enough water to thin it down to a sauce consistency (about 2–3 tablespoons). Taste and adjust the garlic and lemon to suit your taste.

Store in an airtight container in the fridge for up to a week.

Na-na wa jorz

MINT & WALNUT SAUCE

MAKES ABOUT 150 G (¾ CUP)

_____

large handful of mint
60 ml (¼ cup) extra virgin olive oil
½ teaspoon salt flakes
½ teaspoon freshly ground black pepper
25 g (¼ cup) walnuts

_____

I created this sauce to serve as an accompaniment to the lamb skewers at Almond Bar. I came up with the idea when I saw just how much mint my mother has in her garden – about four different patches. Suffice to say, Carol and I are eternally grateful as we go through quite a bit in the restaurant. Walnuts are used in many traditional Middle Eastern dishes, mostly as a topping, but why not create a simple Arab pesto with them that works well with lamb? It can also be used as a marinade.

Place the mint, olive oil, salt and pepper in a small food processor and process until combined. Add the walnuts and process to the desired consistency – you can choose to leave the walnuts in larger pieces or blend a little longer for a smoother sauce.

Store in an airtight container in the fridge for up to 10 days.

Clockwise from top left: *Dad, Carol, Aunty Azizi, Aunty Adele and Mum*

Toum

GARLIC PASTE

MAKES ABOUT 350 G (2½ CUPS), ALTHOUGH
THE QUANTITIES CAN BE HALVED

---

30 cloves garlic
2 teaspoons salt flakes
2 tablespoons lemon juice
400 ml (1⅔ cups) vegetable oil

Note: Although it may seem logical to use
olive oil, it is not appropriate for this recipe
as it will take away from the kick of the
garlic. The lighter flavour of vegetable oil
is a better match.

The origin of this rich garlic paste is unknown, but it is very
popular across the Levant region, made up of Syria, Lebanon,
Jordan, the Palestinian territories, and Israel. It is most commonly
eaten as part of a barbecue, with chicken. The following recipe is
the heart-stopping, sleep-depriving, water-guzzling, tear-jerking
version that I grew up with. As kids, Mum often asked my sister
and me (okay, maybe Carol more than me, as she is older) to crush
garlic for her with a wooden mortar and pestle so she could make
toum ever so carefully by hand. Thank God for food processors!

Peel the garlic cloves, ensuring all outer layers are completely
removed. (My mum believes that soaking unpeeled garlic in warm
water aids the peeling process without compromising the flavour of
the garlic, which can happen if the cloves are cracked to remove the
skin. I must admit, I'm usually a bit lazy and crack the skin . . .)

Place the peeled cloves in a food processor with the salt and
lemon juice and process until the garlic is as finely chopped as
possible. With the motor running, slowly pour in a steady stream
of vegetable oil. The key is to ensure you don't add too much oil
at once, and allow the oil you have poured in to be absorbed into the
toum before continuing the stream. Once all the oil has been used,
add 1 tablespoon water to slightly thin the paste. The toum can be
stored in the fridge in an airtight container for up to 3 weeks.

THE AUSSIE TOUM

MAKES ABOUT 300 G (1½ CUPS)

---

12 cloves garlic
2 tablespoons extra virgin olive oil
1 egg
1 tablespoon lemon juice
2 teaspoons Dijon mustard
½ teaspoon salt flakes
1 teaspoon freshly ground black pepper
250 ml (1 cup) vegetable oil

When we opened the restaurant, Carol and I put a lot of thought
into the accompaniments, as they are just as important as the
mains. The obvious one for char-grilled chicken skewers would
have to be toum, but how would people react to it? We were
worried it might be too overwhelming, so we opted for the next
best thing – toum with a little homemade mayonnaise. It was
a big hit, and we still give customers the option of what we call
'real toum' or this toned-down version.

Start by peeling the garlic and crushing it into a bowl with a garlic
crusher. Drizzle with the olive oil and set aside.

To make the mayonnaise, place the egg, lemon juice, mustard,
salt and pepper in a small food processor and process until well
combined. With the motor running, add the vegetable oil in a very
slow, thin stream until the mixture is creamy and all the oil has
been incorporated.

Once the mayonnaise is ready, add the garlic and olive oil
mixture to the processor and blend until well combined and the
garlic oil is no longer visible around the side of the processor bowl.
Store in an airtight container in the fridge for up to 1 week.

Na-na bi jibneh bay-da: 'Minty'

MINT & FETA DIP

MAKES ABOUT 375 G (1 CUP)

---

350 g (12 oz) sheep's milk feta
2 teaspoons dried mint
2 tablespoons lemon juice
Middle Eastern bread, to serve

White cheeses are often mixed with fresh or dried herbs as part of the breakfast or mezza table. This is a very simple but tasty dip that can also be used as a sandwich spread or, mixed with a little olive oil, as a salad dressing. My cousin Tony was so obsessed with minty that at one stage he ate it not only as a dip, but also with chicken skewers and savoury pastries.

Crumble the feta into a small food processor by hand, ensuring there are no large chunks. Add the mint and lemon juice and process until a thick paste is formed and the mixture is smooth and well combined. Serve with Middle Eastern bread.

Store in an airtight container in the fridge for up to 1 week.

Basal, banadora wa sumac makhloot

ONION, TOMATO & SUMAC RELISH

MAKES ABOUT 415 G (1 CUP)

---

3 red onions, roughly chopped
small handful of flat-leaf parsley, finely chopped
1 tablespoon ground sumac
60 ml (¼ cup) extra virgin olive oil
1 teaspoon salt flakes
110 g (½ cup) sugar
1 teaspoon ground cumin
5 cloves, crushed
2 ripe tomatoes, roughly chopped

Kafta (see page 118) is traditionally served with a red onion, parsley and sumac salad. I found that this was a bit hit and miss in the restaurant so I adapted the ingredients to make a relish instead – luckily, it seems to be a success. This relish is a beautiful accompaniment to all meat dishes, but it's also great on wraps and sandwiches and with omelettes.

Place the onion, parsley and sumac in a medium bowl and mix together well.

Heat the olive oil in a medium saucepan over medium–high heat for about 3 minutes. Add the onion mixture and stir to coat in the oil. Stir in the salt, sugar, cumin and cloves until well combined.

Add the tomato and mix well, then reduce the heat to low and simmer gently for about 20 minutes, stirring every few minutes.

Remove the relish from the heat and leave to cool completely. Store in an airtight container in the fridge for up to 2 weeks.

Shawandar

BEETROOT DIP

MAKES ABOUT 200 G (1 CUP)

———————————

3 beetroots (beets) or 5 baby beets
60 ml (¼ cup) olive oil
55 g (¼ cup) sugar
1 teaspoon ground cumin
1 teaspoon ground coriander
1 teaspoon ground cinnamon
1 teaspoon sweet paprika
½ teaspoon salt flakes
60 ml (¼ cup) lemon juice
2 teaspoons natural yoghurt
Middle Eastern bread, to serve

———————————

I rediscovered my love for beetroot (beet) a few years ago at a friend's barbecue, when baby beets were served with steak and salad. I decided to roast some beetroot (beet) and create a dip with a little Syrian flair. Shawandar is full of flavour and can be enjoyed as a dip on its own, but I also love to put a big dollop on top of barbecued steak. If you're worried about staining your hands when you prepare the beetroot (beet), slip on a pair of prep gloves before you start.

Preheat the oven to 200°C (fan)/425°F/gas mark 7.

Wash the beetroots (beets) under cold water, rubbing the skin with your hands to remove any loose dirt. Cut off the top stalks of the beetroot, leaving about 2 cm (¾ in) of the stalk to keep the juices in during roasting. Leave the bottom tail intact.

Place the beetroots (beets) on a baking tray (cookie sheet) and pour the olive oil over them. Using your hands, gently toss to ensure each beetroot (beet) is coated in oil. Cook the beetroots (beets) for 1½ hours or until tender, turning them every 20 minutes or so. Test by pricking the middle of a beetroot (beet) with a fork – if it slides off the fork fairly quickly it's ready. Remove from the oven and leave to cool for about 15 minutes.

Remove the top and bottom ends of the beetroots (beets) and discard. The skin should be easy enough to slip off by hand. Cut the peeled beetroots (beets) into large cubes.

Place the cubed beetroot (beet), sugar, cumin, coriander, cinnamon, paprika, salt and lemon juice in a food processor and process until the ingredients are well combined but there is still some texture to the dip. This will take about 3–5 minutes, depending on the firmness of the roast beetroot (beet). Halfway through, scrape down the sides of the bowl and check there are no large chunks of beetroot (beet) in the mix. Finally, add the yoghurt and process until just combined and the dip becomes a slightly brighter purple colour.

The dip can be served immediately while still a little warm, or you may want to refrigerate it for about half an hour if you prefer it slightly chilled. Serve with Middle Eastern bread.

Store in an airtight container in the fridge for up to 5 days.

Muhammara

CHARGRILLED PEPPER, WALNUT & POMEGRANATE DIP

MAKES 360 G (1½ CUPS)

———————

3 red (bell) peppers

2 cloves garlic, peeled and left whole

1 tablespoon ground cumin

1 tablespoon sweet paprika

1 teaspoon dried chilli flakes

60 ml (¼ cup) lemon juice

2½ tablespoons extra virgin olive oil

2½ tablespoons pomegranate molasses

35 g (⅓ cup) walnuts

25 g (¼ cup) dried breadcrumbs

Middle Eastern bread, to serve

———————

This amazing dip, which originated in Aleppo, is very dear to my heart. Known for its spicy kick, walnut crunch and subtle pomegranate molasses flavour, it's also beautiful as a spread or marinade. I chargrill the red peppers to give the dip a little more texture and a good earthy flavour.

Place the whole peppers under a hot grill (broiler) and cook, turning, until the skin is almost black. Remove from the grill (broiler) and allow to cool completely. Pull the skin away from the flesh and remove the stalks and seeds.

Place the pepper flesh, garlic, spices, lemon juice, olive oil and pomegranate molasses in a food processor. Pulse until the ingredients are just combined but not completely smooth – the pepper flesh should be roughly chopped but still visible.

Finally, add the walnuts and breadcrumbs and pulse briefly until combined. The walnuts need to remain chunky. The dip should be thick and moist, and a deep, earthy red colour.

Serve with Middle Eastern bread.

Store in an airtight container in the fridge for up to 5 days.

Note

For muhammara labne, add 280 g (1 cup) labne (see page 28) to the above recipe and mix until creamy orange in colour and well combined.

Labne

DRIED YOGHURT DIP

MAKES ABOUT 800 G (3½ CUPS)

---

3 teaspoons salt flakes

1.12 kg (4 cups) Greek-style yoghurt
(or if you're really game, make your own yoghurt –
see page 47)

olive oil, to cover

When I was growing up, you were unlikely to find labne at the local grocer and, if you did, it wasn't as good as the homemade version. Nowadays, there are numerous varieties to choose from, including marinated labne balls, labne mixed with olives and peppers and so on. I am truly blessed, though, to have a mother who has never let the fridge go without labne for as long as I can remember. Going home to Mum and Dad's, at times arriving in the early hours of the morning after work, the first thing I see hanging off their balcony railing is my old university library bag, which Mum uses to drain the yoghurt, with a bucket underneath to catch the whey.

Labne is most commonly used as a spread on a wrap. It is also a very popular condiment that can be used instead of sour cream on soups or dolloped on top of steak.

Stir the salt through the yoghurt, then place the yoghurt in a muslin (cheesecloth) bag or large clean jay cloth. Bring the corners of the cloth or the top open end of the bag together and tie it closed. Hang the yoghurt at room temperature over a sink with a bowl sitting underneath to catch the whey from the yoghurt.

For best results, leave the yoghurt to drain for at least 15 hours; after this time it will be wonderfully thick and creamy. Spoon the labne into an airtight container and store in the fridge, covered with a thin layer of olive oil or with a damp piece of kitchen paper (paper towel) to avoid mould. It should keep for about 2 weeks.

Note

Another way to prepare the labne is to line the base of a colander or large plastic sieve with a few sheets of thick good-quality kitchen paper (paper towel) and sit the colander or sieve over a large container. Spoon the yoghurt and salt mixture onto the kitchen paper (paper towel) and leave it to drain.

To make lab'tar, place 280 g (1 cup) labne, 135 g (¾ cup) za'atar (see page 12) and 2 tablespoons extra virgin olive oil in a bowl and mix until well combined.

Labne balls can be made if the labne is left to drain for about 30 hours, so it becomes even thicker, with a slight sourness to it. Remove the labne from the bag or cloth and, using clean hands that have been lightly coated in olive oil, shape into 2–3 cm (¾–1¼ in) balls. The labne balls can then be rolled in your choice of dried oregano, mint, za'atar (see page 12), sesame seeds, freshly ground black pepper or chilli flakes. Pack into a glass jar and cover completely with extra virgin olive oil. Store in a cool cupboard away from sunlight for up to 1 month.

Avotamor

CREAMY DATE & AVOCADO DIP

MAKES ABOUT 350 G (2 CUPS)

———————————

140 g (1 cup) roughly chopped pitted dates
3 ripe avocados
140 g (½ cup) tahini
½ teaspoon salt flakes
½ teaspoon freshly ground black pepper
juice of 2 lemons
Middle Eastern bread, to serve

———————————

Beautiful dates are available all year round at Middle Eastern grocers. They are eaten as snacks, served to guests and commonly found in Middle Eastern sweets (candies). Here the combination of sweet dates with creamy avocado and tahini is a real winner.

Place the dates, avocado flesh, tahini, salt and pepper in a food processor and mix together until combined. Add the lemon juice and mix again. The mixture will thicken slightly, so add about 80 ml (⅓ cup) water to thin it down to the desired consistency. Add more water if you like, but pour it in gradually so the dip doesn't become too runny. Taste and adjust the seasoning if necessary.

Serve with fresh or fried Middle Eastern bread.

Store in an airtight container in the fridge for up to 4 days.

Batata

POTATO & ARISH BALLS

SERVES 4

———————————

4 large maincrop or Russet potatoes,
peeled and cut into 2–3 cm (¾–1¼ in) cubes

2 teaspoons salt flakes

1 teaspoon freshly ground black pepper

75 g (½ cup) plain (all-purpose) flour

80 ml (⅓ cup) milk

1 egg

100 g (1 cup) dried breadcrumbs

2 tablespoons arish cheese (see page 47)

250 ml (1 cup) olive oil

natural yoghurt, for dipping (optional)

———————————

This Almond Bar speciality combines some of my favourite ingredients and cooking methods all in one mouthful. Dinner at home was always accompanied by potatoes or rice. So I decided to create what looks like a mini arancini ball with Mum's beloved arish cheese, crumbed and then fried for a golden delight. Use gorgonzola dolce cheese if arish is not available, or mix your favourite crumbly cheese with 1 teaspoon sweet paprika and ½ teaspoon dried chilli flakes.

Place the potato cubes in a medium saucepan and cover with water. Bring to the boil, then reduce the heat to medium and cook for 15–20 minutes or until the potato is tender enough to mash. Drain and set aside to cool.

Place the potato in a bowl with the salt, pepper, 1 tablespoon flour and 1 tablespoon milk and mash all the ingredients together. You don't want the mixture to be too wet as it needs to be shaped into firm balls.

Make an egg wash by whisking together the egg and remaining milk in a small bowl.

Place the remaining flour in a separate bowl and the breadcrumbs in a third bowl. The arish should be ready for use in its own bowl.

Place all the bowls close to one another in a circle with a clean flat plate in the centre for the finished product.

Roll the potato mixture into 4 cm (1½ in) balls (you should get about eight balls out of this mix). Stick your index finger halfway into the centre of each potato ball to create a small hole. Place about 1 teaspoon arish in each hole, then close the potato around the filling and re-roll the ball between your palms.

Coat each ball lightly with flour, them dip it in the egg wash before covering liberally with breadcrumbs. As you finish each ball, place it on the clean plate.

Heat the olive oil in a shallow frying pan (skillet) over medium heat. Add half the potato balls and cook, turning once, until golden brown. Remove and drain on kitchen paper (paper towels). Repeat with the remaining balls. Allow to cool for about 5 minutes before serving, as they will be piping hot on the inside. Serve with natural yoghurt for dipping, if you like.

bi arush

Manoosh

ZA'ATAR PIZZAS

SERVES 6

---

250 g (1⅔ cups) plain (all-purpose) flour, plus extra if needed

2 teaspoons salt flakes

20 g (¾ oz) dried yeast

2 teaspoons sugar

80 ml (⅓ cup) vegetable oil

80 g (½ cup) za'atar (see page 12)

150 ml (⅔ cup) olive oil

As a baby I apparently started eating manoosh before any other solids – this shows how long manoosh has been in my life! There are many Middle Eastern bakeries that specialise in breakfast pizzas. No matter which one you visit, they will all tell you their most popular product is manoosh, a thin crust topped with a layer of za'atar spice mixed with oil. But why buy them when it is so easy to make your own?

Put the flour, salt and yeast in a bowl and mix together with your hands, rubbing the ingredients between your palms. Add the sugar, vegetable oil and about 60 ml (¼ cup) warm water. Bring the mixture together, then turn it out onto a floured surface and knead for about 10 minutes to make a firm, smooth dough, adding more flour if necessary. Gently shape the dough into a ball, then cover and rest at room temperature for about 1 hour.

Preheat the oven to 200°C (fan)/425°F/gas mark 7. Line baking trays (cookies sheets) or pizzas trays with baking paper (you need enough space to fit six 20 cm/8 in round pizzas).

Pull off six sections of dough slightly smaller in size than a tennis ball and roll out to a 20 cm (8 in) round, about 3–4 mm (⅛ in) thick. Make a slight border by pressing your fingers around the edge of each round.

Mix the za'atar with the olive oil to form a smooth paste, then spread it evenly over the pizza bases.

Slide the bases onto the trays and bake for 10–15 minutes or until the bases are golden brown.

Note

Manoosh can be enjoyed just as they are or served with labne (see page 28), fresh mint leaves, sliced cucumber and tomato, olives or pickled turnip. Either serve them as an accompaniment or arrange them over one half of the cooked pizza and fold the other half over the top.

Haloumi wa beid o' baba ghanouj

FRIED HALOUMI WITH BOILED EGG & BABA GHANOUJ

SERVES 4

---

1 tomato, finely diced
100 g (generous ⅓ cup) baba ghanouj (see page 16)
250 g (9 oz) good-quality haloumi
2 tablespoons olive oil
1 teaspoon dried oregano
2 hard-boiled eggs, peeled and each cut into 5 slices
2 tablespoons chopped flat-leaf parsley

Although haloumi is traditionally eaten fresh in the Middle East, Arabs also love this salty cheese cooked. While it tastes very good on its own, the true flavour of cooked haloumi is always enhanced by its accompaniment, which should remove some of the salty flavour, and highlight how light the (traditional) combination of sheep's and goat's milk can actually be.

Mix together the tomato and baba ghanouj in a small bowl.

Remove the haloumi from the packet and wash under cold water to remove excess salt in the brine. Cut the haloumi into 10 slices.

Have your serving plate ready so that once the haloumi is cooked you can assemble the dish immediately.

Heat the olive oil in a medium–large frying pan (skillet) over medium heat. Place all the haloumi slices in the pan (if you cannot cook them all at once, do it in two batches). As the haloumi starts frying, sprinkle each slice with oregano (you will only need to do this on one side.) As soon as one side starts to turn golden brown, turn the haloumi over and cook the other side – keep a close eye on it as it can dry out very quickly if overcooked.

As soon as the other side is golden, remove the haloumi from the pan and arrange on the serving plate, oregano-side up. Place a slice of egg on each piece, followed by a teaspoon of the baba ghanouj and tomato mixture. Finish with a sprinkling of chopped parsley, then serve immediately.

Basturma, betinjen, batata o' shawandar

BASTURMA STACK

SERVES 4

---

1 beetroot (beet), washed and cut into quarters

½ aubergine (eggplant), peeled, cut in half lengthways and cut into 5 mm (¼ in) thick slices

1 teaspoon salt flakes

250 ml (1 cup) olive oil

1 maincrop or Russet potato, peeled and cut widthways into 5 mm (¼ in) thick slices

¼ cucumber, finely diced

½ teaspoon dried mint

2 tablespoons natural yoghurt

8 slices basturma

My parents often took us to parties, weddings, christenings and all sorts of functions held in reception centres specialising in Middle Eastern cuisine. One of the highlights (okay, maybe the highlight) of these functions was that we were able to gorge ourselves on overflowing plates of mezza that were constantly being replenished. My brother Steven and I often fought over the hummus and fried bread, but my favourite dish was the beautiful basturma, a type of dried beef coated in spices. Here I have added a couple of other ingredients; this dish works well as a light snack or as a swanky addition to the mezza table.

Place the beetroot (beet) in a small saucepan and cover with water. Bring to the boil, then reduce the heat and simmer for 15–20 minutes or until tender. Drain and set aside to cool. Once the beetroot (beet) is cool, peel then cut into 5 mm (¼ in) thick slices and refrigerate.

Meanwhile, arrange the aubergine (eggplant) slices on a piece of kitchen paper (paper towel) and sprinkle with ½ teaspoon salt. Set aside for 20 minutes so the salt can draw out excess moisture, then rinse and pat dry.

Heat the olive oil in a small frying pan (skillet) over medium-high heat and fry the potato slices until golden on both sides and tender in the middle. Remove and drain on kitchen paper (paper towels). Add the aubergine (eggplant) slices and fry until golden brown on both sides. Remove and drain on kitchen paper (paper towels).

Mix together the cucumber, mint and yoghurt in a small bowl. Set aside.

Arrange the basturma slices on a serving plate. Layer the potato slices over the basturma and season with a pinch of salt. Place the beetroot (beet) on top of the potato, followed by the sliced aubergine (eggplant) as the final layer. Finish the dish with a dollop of the cucumber yoghurt and serve immediately.

Scallops wa basturma

SCALLOPS & BASTURMA DRIZZLED WITH POMEGRANATE BUTTER

SERVES 6

---

125 ml (½ cup) vegetable oil

6 × 5 mm (¼ in) thick slices aubergine (eggplant),
cut in half

2 tablespoons olive oil

12 fresh scallops, roe removed

12 slices basturma

POMEGRANATE BUTTER

80 g (5½ tablespoons) butter, diced and softened at
room temperature

1 teaspoon pomegranate molasses

¼ teaspoon crushed garlic

½ teaspoon freshly ground black pepper

1 teaspoon lemon juice

This recipe came about because I wanted to create a seafood dish with contrasting flavours that work perfectly together. To give it a Middle Eastern touch, I added a little pomegranate and basturma. They taste beautiful with the scallops.

To make the pomegranate butter, place all the ingredients in a food processor and mix until combined. Set aside at room temperature.

Heat the vegetable oil in a medium frying pan (skillet) over medium heat, add the aubergine (eggplant) slices and cook until golden brown on both sides. Remove and drain on kitchen paper (paper towels).

Heat the olive oil in a small frying pan (skillet) over medium-high heat and cook the scallops for about 2 minutes on each side to seal. Take care not to overcook them. Set aside.

To assemble, start with the basturma at the bottom, followed by the aubergine (eggplant) and then the scallops. Finally, place a small dollop of pomegranate butter on top of each scallop and allow it to melt. Serve immediately.

o' zibdet dibis

Kibbet

PUMPKIN KIBBEH

MAKES ABOUT 20

---

800 g (1¾ lb) butternut pumpkin (squash), peeled and cut into large cubes

1 brown onion

300 g (2 cups) fine white burghul (bulgur wheat)

1 tablespoon salt flakes

1 teaspoon freshly ground black pepper

180 g (1¼ cups) plain (all-purpose) flour, plus extra if needed

500 ml (2 cups) vegetable or corn oil

chopped mint or lemon juice stirred through natural yoghurt, to serve

STUFFING

75 g (½ cup) dried split chickpeas

2 tablespoons olive oil

1 small brown onion, finely chopped

¼ red (bell) pepper, seeds and membrane removed, flesh finely diced

½ small carrot, grated

small handful of flat-leaf parsley, finely chopped

50 g (½ cup) roughly chopped walnuts

2 teaspoons seven-spice mix (see page 13)

1½ teaspoons freshly ground black pepper

1 teaspoon salt flakes

The main ingredient in this vegan dish is my favourite vegetable: pumpkin. I never thought kibbeh could taste so good without the meat it's usually made with, but these little torpedoes certainly proved me wrong.

To make the stuffing, soak the chickpeas in a large bowl of water overnight. Drain. They should be soft but still have a slight crunch.

Heat the olive oil in a large frying pan (skillet) over medium heat, add the onion and cook until translucent. Stir in the chickpeas, pepper, carrot, parsley and walnuts, then add the spice mix and seasoning and fry for a few minutes. Remove from the heat and let the stuffing cool. It will sit happily in the fridge for a day or two until you are ready to make the kibbeh.

Place the pumpkin in a medium saucepan and cover with cold water. Bring to the boil over medium heat, then reduce the heat and simmer for 25–30 minutes or until nicely softened. Drain and set aside to cool for about 20 minutes.

Grate the onion and strain. Place it in a large bowl with the burghul (bulgur wheat) and add the salt, pepper, flour and pumpkin. Gently bring the mixture together – you are looking for a dough-like consistency, but it shouldn't be as thick and dry. Add a little more flour if needed to create a more pliable dough, then taste and add more salt and pepper if liked. Place the pumpkin dough in the fridge for about 2 hours to chill and rest.

Fill a bowl with lukewarm water and set it by your side. Moisten your hands, then grab a golf-ball-sized portion of dough and roll it into a smooth ball. With the index finger of one hand, poke a hole in it while cupping it with the other palm; gently move your index finger back and forth to form a long and narrow cavity inside the ball. Spoon in about 1 teaspoon of the stuffing, then close the opening by patching it and creating a point. Roll the kibbeh between your moist palms or on a hard surface to make it look smooth and elongated at the ends. Repeat with the remaining kibbeh mixture and stuffing.

When all the kibbeh have been formed, store them on a tray in the fridge while you get the oil ready. The uncooked kibbeh can actually be stored in the freezer for about a month if you want to have some ready for another occasion.

Heat the vegetable or corn oil in a medium heavy-based saucepan to 170°C/338°F (or until a cube of bread browns in 20 seconds). Add three or four kibbeh at a time (so you don't overcrowd the pan) and cook for 3–4 minutes or until they are lightly golden and crisp. Remove with a slotted spoon and drain on kitchen paper (paper towels).

Serve hot or at room temperature with mint or lemon yoghurt or simply with a squeeze of lemon juice.

Makdoos

STUFFED & PICKLED MINI AUBERGINES

MAKES 12–15

2 tablespoons salt flakes
1 kg (2¼ lb) very small, thin aubergines (eggplants), stems removed
500 ml (2 cups) extra virgin olive oil

STUFFING
120 g (1 cup) finely chopped walnuts
4 small chillies, finely chopped (or to taste)
6 cloves garlic, crushed
1 tablespoon salt flakes

From a very young age I used to watch my mother pickling and stuffing all sorts of vegetables. One that really stood out was her stuffed aubergine (eggplant), or makdoos. Originating in Syria, makdoos are something the Salloum household never goes without. Traditionally a part of the breakfast table, makdoos are beautiful on their own, with some fresh white cheese or even folded through a salad. Take care when choosing the aubergines (eggplants) for this: they should be 5–6 cm (2–2½ in) long and mostly purple or speckled purple and white.

Bring a large saucepan of water to the boil and add 1 tablespoon salt. Poach the aubergines (eggplants) over medium heat for 10–15 minutes or until softened. Remove and place in a sieve set over a large bowl. Put a plate on the aubergines (eggplants) and weigh it down with a stone or half a brick. Leave the aubergines (eggplants) to drain for about 2 hours.

Remove the plate, then very gently squeeze the aubergines (eggplants) to get rid of any excess water. Cut a slit down the length of each aubergine (eggplant) (without cutting all the way through), leaving the ends intact so as to form a pocket. Put a pinch of the remaining salt in each pocket and close it. Return the aubergines (eggplants) to the sieve and weigh them down as before. Drain for a further 2 hours, then squeeze gently again to remove any remaining water.

To make the stuffing, mix together all the ingredients in a bowl.

Spoon some stuffing into each pocket and gently close. Place the stuffed aubergines (eggplants) in an airtight jar, stacking them around the inside of the jar so they fit snugly. Cover them completely with olive oil, then secure the lid and place in a dark cupboard at room temperature. They should be ready to eat in 7 days. Check the jar from time to time to make sure the level of the olive oil hasn't reduced too much. If it has, pour in enough oil to cover the aubergines (eggplants) to prevent mould developing.

MAKING THE AMAZING
ARISH CHEESE & SHANKLISH

THE 'BLUE CHEESE' OF THE MIDDLE EAST

The process of making arish cheese and shanklish has itsorigins in Tartous, Syria, and I'll warn you upfront that the traditional method is time-consuming and labour-intensive. However, nothing compares to the end result. The commercially available product is good but, like many things, it's just not the same as making your own.

I know this from a lifetime of experience. When I was growing up I would often open a cupboard or a cooled oven to find the odd, grey-brown cheese fermenting away. What is available in shops labelled as shanklish is a lovely crumbly mature cheese that is sometimes lightly spiced with chilli and usually coated in dried oregano. The two couldn't be more different.

The whole process only really requires 2 litres (8 cups) fresh cow's milk, 280 g (1 cup) natural yoghurt and a little bit of salt. If you like a bit of heat, a couple of small chopped red chillies work well, along with a good sprinkling of sweet paprika. For those wanting to coat their shanklish, you will need 90 g (½ cup) za'atar (see page 12) or dried oregano.

First, you must bring the milk to the boil in a large saucepan, stirring constantly. As soon as it comes to the boil, remove it from the heat and leave it to cool to the point where you can stick your finger in it without burning yourself. Now you can stir in the yoghurt and about a teaspoon of salt.

Cover the pan with its lid, then wrap it tightly with a blanket and leave it at room temperature (away from direct sunlight) for 12–14 hours. When you remove the lid, you will see that you've made natural yoghurt, which can be stored in the fridge for about a week. I have watched my mother make yoghurt this way since I was 5 years old.

If you have already refrigerated the yoghurt, remove it from the fridge and leave it at room temperature for about 2 hours. Thoroughly rinse out a large elongated earthenware jug (pitcher) or vase with plenty of water – it's important to do this or it will soak up a lot of liquid during the preparation process. My mother told me that prior to the use of clay, people would make bags from cow hide to store the yoghurt! Place the yoghurt in the jug or vase, then pour in 1.5–2 litres (6 ⅓–8 cups) water. Securely cover the opening of the jug (pitcher) or vase with a cloth or tea (dish) towel and rock it back and forth to separate the yoghurt from the butter fat. After about 10 minutes of rocking, much of the fat will have risen to the surface.

Continue rocking for about an hour or so. Every 10 minutes, remove the cover to check that the solidified fat has mostly risen to the surface.

When you have finished rocking, use a medium sieve to remove the fat particles that have formed in the yoghurt mixture. This is actually a beautiful butter that can be used like any other good-quality butter, so do not discard it.

The remaining skimmed yoghurt is called 'shen-ineh', which is also used to make the yoghurt drink we know as 'Ayran'. Transfer it to a saucepan and cook over medium heat until it just starts to boil. When this happens, remove the pan from the heat and leave the shen-ineh to cool to room temperature.

Place the cooled shen-ineh in a cloth bag, such as a muslin (cheesecloth) bag or an old, thin pillowcase (my mother uses my old uni library bag!). You now want to hang it somewhere to drain for 24–30 hours. Some people will leave the bag hanging off a tap over a sink. My mother fluctuates between the tap option, hanging it off the balcony railing with an empty container underneath to catch the drips, and sitting the bag in a large colander over a container. Whatever you choose, the result of this draining process is beautiful arish cheese. If you like, you can season your arish by stirring through a little more salt, sweet paprika and/or chilli.

To make shanklish, roll the arish into 4 cm (1½ in) balls and place on a tray, plate or chopping board lined with a clean tea (dish) towel. Cover with a light mesh cloth (to keep bugs away) and leave in the sun for about 7 days, taking it inside overnight. This is where the ageing process begins. Some people will stop and eat the cheese after this step – if you are going to do this, it's a good idea to roll the cheese in za'atar or dried oregano before serving. Delicious!

For the real deal, the aging process continues . . .

The next step is to place the cheese balls in an airtight jar in a dark cupboard. A method my mother uses to age the cheese just that little bit faster is to place each ball in a small plastic freezer bag. She then leaves them to mature for at least 2 weeks. After this final step, they can be removed and eaten. She washes off the mould under cold water, then slices the cheese and drizzles it liberally with a good olive oil. You can also coat the washed shanklish with oregano or za'atar. It is then enjoyed at any time of the day.

This is the real shanklish cheese. I didn't say it was going to be easy, but the end result is remarkable.

Above: *Dad and family friend George Jarouge share the rocking process*

Below: *George pours the yoghurt and water into the earthenware vase*

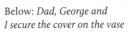

Below: *Dad, George and I secure the cover on the vase*

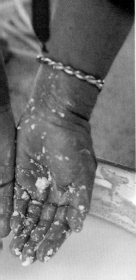

Shared plates

Ma'aneq bi hindbi

MIDDLE EASTERN SAUSAGES WITH CHICORY & FENNEL

MAKES ABOUT 30

---

2 × 420 g (15 oz) cans diced tomato

1 teaspoon salt flakes

1 teaspoon dried chilli flakes

55 g (¼ cup) sugar

1 bunch chicory (endive), stalks removed, leaves roughly chopped

½ fennel bulb, trimmed and thinly sliced

SAUSAGES

300 g (11 oz) finely minced (ground) lamb

300 g (11 oz) finely minced (ground) beef

1 teaspoon ground cumin

1 teaspoon ground coriander

1 teaspoon freshly grated nutmeg

2½ teaspoons salt flakes

1 teaspoon crushed fenugreek seeds

1 teaspoon sweet paprika

1 teaspoon ground cinnamon

1 teaspoon freshly ground black pepper

1 teaspoon freshly ground white pepper

½ teaspoon ground cloves

60 ml (¼ cup) white vinegar

60 g (4 tablespoons) butter

1 bundle small sheep casings

2 tablespoons olive oil

These little spiced sausages are another jewel of the Levant. They are low in fat and easy to bake in the oven, avoiding the splatter from frying and the thin layer of fat that sits on the roof of your mouth when you eat some sausages. At home, ma'aneq were often teamed with a side of mashed potatoes and a big green salad. Okay, I admit we occasionally added tomato sauce. As an adult, I came up with a classier spiced tomato sauce, which I have included here.

Bundles of casings used for sausages can be ordered and purchased through most butchers. Ask for advice on how many you'll need to make about 30 sausages about 7–8 cm (2¾–3¼ in) in length. The cheat's option is to purchase these beautiful little sausages from a good Middle Eastern butcher. They come in mild or hot, and sometimes have extra flavourings added.

To make the sausages, place all the ingredients (except the casings and olive oil) in a large bowl and mix until well combined. Leave in the fridge for about half an hour.

In the meantime, wash the casings under cold water to remove any excess salt. Leave them to dry on a clean tea (dish) towel.

To assemble the sausages, cut the casings into 35 cm (14 in) lengths, then tie one end of each length of casing into a knot to close. Spoon some of the sausage filling into a piping (pastry) bag fitted with a 1 cm (½ in) wide nozzle. Place the open end of one of the casings around the nozzle (tip) and hold with one hand. With the other hand, squeeze the piping bag to push the mixture into the casing – you want each sausage to be 7–8 cm (2¾–3¼ in) in length. Twist the casing to close each sausage, then tie the end once the whole casing has been filled. Repeat with the remaining sausage mix and casings to make about 30 sausages.

Preheat the oven to 190°C (fan)/400°F/gas mark 6.

Place the sausages on a non-stick baking tray (cookie sheet), drizzle with the olive oil and cook on the middle shelf for about 30 minutes or until browned. Cover with foil and cook for another 10–15 minutes.

Meanwhile, combine the tomato, salt, chilli and sugar in a small saucepan and simmer over medium heat, stirring regularly, until the sugar has dissolved. This will take about 10–15 minutes.

Blanch the chicory (endive) and fennel in a saucepan of boiling water to slightly soften. Drain, then spread out on a large serving platter or tray. Follow with the sausages, then pour the tomato sauce over the top.

shemrah

Lilit bi Djej

CHICKEN & SWISS CHARD PARCELS

MAKES 10

---

10 Swiss chard leaves

350 g (12 oz) skinless chicken breast fillet

120 g (½ cup) chargrilled pepper,
walnut and pomegranate dip (see page 26)

1 teaspoon salt flakes

60 ml (¼ cup) olive oil

thinly sliced tomato, to serve

One day I decided to create a leafy parcel with a chicken filling. But what would I add for flavour? It's amazing how much flavour muhammara (chargrilled pepper dip) can bring to a dish. Here it provides texture and a little bite of chilli, without taking away from the flavour of the Swiss chard. This is a very simple dish that doesn't take long to prepare and takes even less time to eat.

Start by removing the hard white stalk that runs through the centre of each Swiss chard leaf. The best way to do this is to cut the leaf into two halves, on either side of the white stalk. Discard the stalk and wash the leaves well to remove any excess dirt.

Bring a medium saucepan of water to the boil and blanch the Swiss chard for about 1 minute. Run the leaves under cold water to refresh and stop the cooking process. Drain, then leave on a clean tea (dish) towel to dry while you prepare the chicken.

Clean and trim the chicken of any fat or cartilage. Thinly slice lengthways to allow for a quick cooking process – the slices should be no more than 5 mm (¼ in) thick. Toss the chicken with the chargrilled pepper dip. Add the salt and 1 tablespoon olive oil and mix until all the chicken pieces are well coated. Cover and marinate in the fridge for about an hour. This will also give the Swiss chard more time to dry.

To make the parcels, flatten out one of the strips of Swiss chard on a chopping board and place about 2 teaspoons of the chicken mixture at one end. Fold over a couple of times to enclose the filling. There should be an opening on either side of the wrapped chicken. Place the partly wrapped chicken, seam-side down, on another half leaf and fold over until the chicken is completely covered and secure in the Swiss chard. Repeat with the remaining leaves and filling.

Heat the remaining olive oil in a medium saucepan over medium heat. Place the parcels in the oil, seam-side down, and cook, covered, for 3 minutes. Turn the parcels over, reduce the heat to low and cook, covered, for a further 4 minutes. Carefully remove from the pan and serve with thinly sliced tomato.

Adas bi hamod

LEMONY LENTIL SOUP

SERVES 4

———————————

5 Swiss chard leaves
60 ml (¼ cup) olive oil
1 brown onion, finely diced
3 cloves garlic, crushed
200 g (1 cup) brown lentils
1 tablespoon salt flakes
1 teaspoon freshly ground black pepper
180 ml (¾ cup) lemon juice
extra virgin olive oil, for drizzling

———————————

There are a few soups with Middle Eastern origins, and this is probably the most well known. The traditional Syrian version includes pomegranate molasses and fresh coriander (cilantro), but what I offer here is the version I grew up with. My parents would break pieces of toasted Middle Eastern bread into their soup bowls to soak up the lemon and garlic flavours.

Remove the hard white stalk that runs through the centre of each Swiss chard leaf and discard. Cut the leaves into 3 mm (⅛ in) thick slices.

Heat 2 tablespoons olive oil in a medium saucepan over medium heat and cook the onion and garlic for about 3 minutes. Reduce the heat to low and sauté for another 5 minutes until softened.

Meanwhile, heat the remaining olive oil in a medium frying pan (skillet) over high heat. Add the Swiss chard and toss for about 4 minutes or until lightly coated with the oil.

Add the Swiss chard to the onion and garlic mixture, then stir in the lentils, salt, pepper, lemon juice and 750 ml (3 cups) water. Cook over low heat for 20–25 minutes or until the lentils have softened. Serve warm with a drizzle of extra virgin olive oil on top.

Shorbet emjadra

LENTIL & BURGHUL SOUP

SERVES 4

————————

400 g (2 cups) brown lentils

320 g (2 cups) coarse burghul (bulgur wheat)

1 teaspoon salt flakes

1 teaspoon freshly ground black pepper

½ head of cauliflower, cut into small florets

180 ml (¾ cup) olive oil

2 brown onions, thinly sliced and cut into half moons

natural yoghurt or crème fraîche, to serve

————————

All children who grew up in a Middle Eastern household know this dish. There are a couple of variations, the main one being that the Lebanese tend to use rice instead of burghul (bulgur wheat). I make it as a nourishing soup, rather than a thicker, more substantial stew.

Rinse the lentils under warm water then place them in a medium saucepan and cover with water. Cook gently over medium–low heat for about 20 minutes or until the lentils have softened but are still firm.

Add the burghul (bulgur wheat) to the lentils, and mix in the salt, pepper and cauliflower. Check the water level and add more if necessary – you want all the ingredients to be completely covered with water, with a little extra liquid on top. Bring to the boil, then cook very slowly over low heat for about 30 minutes, stirring every 5 minutes or so.

Meanwhile, heat the olive oil in a frying pan (skillet) over high heat and cook the onion, stirring constantly, until it is nicely browned and crispy. Remove from the pan and drain on kitchen paper (paper towels).

Serve the soup with a dollop of yoghurt or crème fraîche and a generous sprinkling of fried onion on top.

Fat-tet hummus

CRUSHED CHICKPEAS WITH YOGHURT, ALMONDS & PINE NUTS

SERVES 4

———————

150 g (1 cup) dried chickpeas

1 teaspoon bicarbonate of soda (baking soda)

1 piece of cassia bark or cinnamon stick

2 bay leaves

2 teaspoons salt flakes

150 ml (⅔ cup) vegetable oil

1 piece of Middle Eastern bread, cut into eighths

140 g (½ cup) tahini

60 ml (¼ cup) lemon juice

1 teaspoon freshly ground black pepper

2 cloves garlic, crushed

300–400 g (1–1⅔ cups) natural yoghurt

35 g (¼ cup) flaked (slivered) almonds, roasted

40 g (¼ cup) pine nuts, roasted

extra virgin olive oil, for drizzling

———————

Fatteh is a traditional Damascus breakfast dish, which is also widely popular in the Levant and Egypt. Although the bread is usually either toasted or left to go stale before being used, I prefer to fry it so it keeps its crunchy texture. This dish, alongside a cup of fresh mint tea, is a beautiful way to start the day. My sister is a huge fan, so it would be silly not to have it on our breakfast menu. In fact, she likes it so much that I often worry about whether it will actually make it to the table! You need to soak the chickpeas overnight so start this recipe a day ahead.

Place the chickpeas and bicarbonate of soda (baking soda) in a bowl, cover with water and leave to soak overnight. Drain, then place the chickpeas in a small saucepan and pour in enough water to cover generously. Add the cassia bark or cinnamon and bay leaves, then place over low heat and simmer, covered, for about 40 minutes or until very tender. Just before the chickpeas are done add 1 teaspoon salt. Simmer for another 5 minutes, then remove from the heat and drain, discarding the bark and leaves.

Heat the vegetable oil in a medium frying pan (skillet) and fry the bread for 10–15 seconds each side until golden brown. Remove from the oil and drain on kitchen paper (paper towels).

Place the soft chickpeas, tahini, lemon juice, pepper, garlic and remaining salt in a bowl. Using a wooden spoon, mix the ingredients together, crushing the chickpeas slightly. Add 2–3 tablespoons cold water if you find that the mixture is too thick. It should have a paste-like consistency.

Break the fried bread into large pieces and place in a medium, shallow bowl. Spread the chickpea mix over the bread, then spoon the yoghurt evenly over the top. Sprinkle over the almonds and pine nuts and finish with a drizzle of olive oil. Serve immediately.

Mokh bi toum

GARLIC LAMBS' BRAINS

SERVES 6

———————————

12 lambs' brains

125 ml (½ cup) white vinegar

1½ tablespoons salt flakes

2 bay leaves

½ lemon

3 cardamom pods

1 piece of cassia bark or cinnamon stick

3 cloves garlic, crushed

½ teaspoon dried chilli flakes

juice of 2 lemons

60 ml (¼ cup) extra virgin olive oil

large handful of flat-leaf parsley,
roughly chopped

———————————

I always knew we were having important guests for dinner when Mum brought out the offal (variety meat)! Given that this generally included brains and tongue, I couldn't understand why offal (variety meat) was considered such a special dish. What ten-year-old would? So, one day I decided to try a little of her lambs' brains (when she wasn't looking of course – I wouldn't want her to think I enjoyed it) and I actually did like it. So I decided to put the recipe in this book.

Place the brains in a medium bowl and cover with cold water. Add the vinegar and 1 tablespoon salt and leave to soak for about an hour. Remove and rinse under cold water.

Combine the brains, bay leaves, lemon, cardamom and cassia or cinnamon in a medium saucepan. Cover with water and bring to the boil over medium–high heat. Reduce the heat and simmer for 15–20 minutes or until the brains have turned a white-grey colour and are firm to the touch. Remove from the pan with a slotted spoon, then pull away and discard the membrane around the brains. Return the brains to the hot water to keep warm.

Place the garlic, chilli flakes, lemon juice, olive oil, parsley and remaining salt in a medium bowl and mix together well.

Remove the brains from the hot water and leave to rest on a chopping board for about 5 minutes. Carefully cut the brains into 1–2 cm (½–¾ in) pieces. Add to the bowl with the garlic and lemon mixture and gently toss to coat. Serve warm.

Eajji sujuk

SUJUK OMELETTE

SERVES 4

---

8 eggs

2 teaspoons dried mint

large handful of flat-leaf parsley, roughly chopped

2 teaspoons salt flakes

½ teaspoon freshly ground black pepper

3 spring onions (scallions), thinly sliced

3 cloves, crushed

200 g (7 oz) sujuk, casing removed, cut in half lengthways and thinly sliced

40 g (3 tablespoons) butter

The word 'eajji' means omelette in Arabic. I remember being in kindergarten and my mother sending me to school with eajji in Middle Eastern bread, with a little side of olives. At six years old – you can imagine how mortified I was. Eajji normally consists of eggs, mint, spring onions (scallions), coriander (cilantro) and parsley, but I've modified the recipe slightly by omitting the coriander (cilantro) and adding sujuk (fermented sausage) for a little spice and texture.

Crack the eggs into a bowl and whisk well. Add the mint, parsley, salt, pepper, spring onions (scallions), cloves and sujuk and whisk until well combined and a light froth has formed.

Melt a quarter of the butter in a medium non-stick frying pan (skillet), about 26 cm (10½ in) over medium heat. Pour in a quarter of the egg mixture and tilt the pan to coat the base. Cook until slightly firm underneath, then fold one half of the omelette onto the other half to make a semi-circle. Cook for another 4–5 minutes, then slide the omelette out of the pan onto a serving plate.

Repeat with the remaining butter and egg mixture to make four omelettes in total. Serve warm.

Ra'men fereh

POMEGRANATE QUAIL

SERVES 4

---

60 ml (¼ cup) pomegranate molasses

1 tablespoon ground cumin

1 teaspoon salt flakes

1 teaspoon freshly ground black pepper

60 ml (¼ cup) olive oil

4 large quail, cleaned and cut into quarters using kitchen scissors (discard the wing tips and neck bone)

When I visited Syria at the age of eight, I saw many different ways of preparing food that left me totally awestruck. One that stands out was the cooking of small birds caught during the shooting season. Unlike many children, I actually enjoyed the barbecued birds, and that memory inspired this recipe made with quail and luscious pomegranate molasses.

In a large bowl, mix together the pomegranate molasses, cumin, salt, pepper and 1 tablespoon olive oil until well combined.

Add the quail to the marinade and turn to coat well, then cover and leave to marinate in the fridge for at least 2 hours, but no more than 6 hours.

Heat the remaining olive oil in a large frying pan (skillet) over high heat. Add the quail and sear on one side, then turn them over and reduce the heat to low. Cover with a lid and cook for a few minutes, then increase the heat to high again and give the second side a final searing for a minute or so, until nicely browned.

Transfer the quail to plates or a platter and drizzle over the pan juices. Serve immediately with your choice of salad, rice or vegetables.

ZA'ATAR PRAWNS WITH PUMPKIN MASH

SERVES 6

---

60 g (¼ cup) za'atar (see page 12)
2 tablespoons lemon juice
1 teaspoon salt flakes
1 teaspoon sweet paprika
80 ml (⅓ cup) olive oil
1 kg (2¼ lb) king prawns (shrimp),
peeled and
deveined, tails intact
lemon wedges, to serve

PUMPKIN MASH
1 small butternut pumpkin (squash), peeled,
seeded and cut into large cubes
20 g (1½ tablespoons) butter
140 g (½ cup) natural yoghurt
salt flakes and freshly ground black pepper

Za'atar is traditionally used in Middle Eastern households as a dipping spice and as a spread on thin homemade pizza bases (see page 36). I could never understand why it was so limited. Why weren't we throwing it into many other dishes? And why – especially – hadn't it been combined with seafood? They make a great team. The citrus element from the sumac in the za'atar marries beautifully with the prawns (shrimp), while the golden sesame seeds provide a nice crispness.

Place the za'atar, lemon juice, salt, paprika and 60 ml (¼ cup) olive oil in a large bowl and mix well. Add the prawns (shrimp) and toss to coat well, then cover and marinate in the fridge for about an hour.

Meanwhile, to make the pumpkin mash, put the pumpkin in a medium saucepan, cover with water and bring to the boil. Reduce the heat and simmer for about 15 minutes until the pumpkin is soft enough to mash but not falling apart. Drain and return it to the pan, then add the butter, yoghurt, salt and pepper and mash until smooth and creamy.

Heat the remaining olive oil in a large frying pan (skillet) over high heat. Add the marinated prawns (shrimp) and cook, tossing them around with tongs, for 3–4 minutes. Reduce the heat to medium-low and cook for a further 5 minutes until they feel firm. You don't want to cook the prawns (shrimp) over high heat for the whole time as this will burn the za'atar.

Spread the pumpkin mash on a round or oval serving plate. Stack the prawns (shrimp) on the mash and serve immediately with lemon wedges.

za'atar

Scallops moghrabieh

SEARED SCALLOPS & AGED CHEESE WITH GIANT COUSCOUS

SERVES 6

---

500 g (1 lb 2 oz) moghrabieh
1 tablespoon olive oil
18–24 scallops, roe removed
1 tomato, diced
2 teaspoons salt flakes
1 teaspoon freshly ground black pepper
100 g (3½ oz) mild shanklish cheese (see page 47)
2 tablespoons chopped flat-leaf parsley

Moghrabieh (or giant couscous) is an interesting ingredient. It has a similar texture and flavour to pasta, so it absorbs the flavour of any sauce or accompaniment very well. It is traditionally served stewed, with chickpeas and beef or chicken. Here, I've taken the slightly unconventional step of adding seafood. The scallops and shanklish cheese work perfectly with the moghrabieh to produce a dish that is light, easy and full of flavour. If you can't find shanklish, a good substitute would be blue brie.

Place the moghrabieh in a medium saucepan and pour in enough water to come 2 cm (¾ in) above the couscous. Bring to the boil over medium heat, stirring every couple of minutes to stop the couscous sticking to the bottom of the pan, then reduce the heat to low and simmer gently until most of the water has been absorbed. This should take about 20 minutes. Drain and wash under cold water.

Heat the olive oil in a medium frying pan (skillet) over high heat. Add the scallops and toss for about 2 minutes to lightly sear on both sides. Reduce the heat to low. Add the couscous, tomato, salt and pepper. Crumble the cheese over the top and slowly mix the ingredients together until the cheese melts completely. (You may need to add 2–3 tablespoons water if the couscous starts to stick to the pan.)

Spoon into shallow bowls and serve sprinkled with parsley.

Foul medammas bi beid wa arish

BROAD BEANS WITH EGGS & ARISH

SERVES 6-8

---

2 × 850 g (1 lb 14 oz) cans broad (fava) beans
(labelled 'foul medammas')

1 teaspoon salt flakes

4 cloves garlic, crushed

180 ml (¾ cup) lemon juice

6 eggs

110 g (4 oz) arish cheese (see page 47),
crumbled (or use goat's feta)

small handful of flat-leaf parsley, roughly chopped

1 large tomato, roughly chopped

1 tablespoon extra virgin olive oil

Middle Eastern bread, to serve

I love the traditional Middle Eastern breakfast so much that I convinced my sister to open once a month on a Sunday morning so that our customers could try it. These breakfasts have been a big hit so far. One dish I always feature on the menu is this broad (fava) bean dish; a family breakfast in the Salloum household isn't a family breakfast without it. We grew up with a simple stewed bean dish sprinkled with diced tomato and parsley, drizzled with olive oil and lemon juice. Here is my variation.

Empty the broad (fava) beans and their liquid into a large saucepan and cook over low heat for approximately 30 minutes or until the beans have softened slightly. Mix in the salt, garlic and 125 ml (½ cup) lemon juice and cook for a further 15 minutes.

Crack the eggs into the pan, placing them evenly over the surface. Cover and cook for 15–20 minutes or until the egg whites are set but the yolks are still soft.

Sprinkle the arish cheese over the eggs and serve the parsley, tomato, olive oil and remaining lemon juice separately so everyone can help themselves. Don't forget fresh bread as well!

Em tabli

CHILLED YOGHURT SOUP WITH BARLEY & CHICKPEAS

Some dishes remind me of summer and of coming home from school to a 'pot of gold' in the fridge. This is certainly one of them. My mother used to make this for us as soon as it started to get warm. I loved the pearl barley in this dish so much that I'd eat all the chickpeas first so I could savour the barley at the end. Start this recipe the night before you want to serve it.

200 g (1 cup) dried chickpeas
300 g (1½ cups) pearl barley, rinsed thoroughly to remove any grit
840 g (3 cups) natural yoghurt
2–3 teaspoons salt flakes
ground sumac, to garnish

Soak the chickpeas in a large bowl of water overnight. Rinse and drain.

Place the chickpeas in a medium saucepan with 750 ml (3 cups) water and bring to the boil. Reduce the heat to medium–low and cook for about 40 minutes or until the chickpeas are tender and can be crushed between two fingers. Drain and allow to cool for 30 minutes.

Meanwhile, place the barley in a small saucepan, cover generously with water and cook over medium–low heat for 30–40 minutes or until the barley has softened and can be crushed between two fingers. Drain and cool for 30 minutes.

Place the yoghurt, salt and 625 ml (2½ cups) water in a large bowl and whisk until combined. Stir in the chickpeas and barley.

Refrigerate for about 4 hours, then serve lightly sprinkled with sumac.

Falafel

CHICKPEA PATTIES

MAKES ABOUT 18

---

150 g (¾ cup) large dried chickpeas

small handful of flat-leaf parsley,
stalks removed

small handful of coriander (cilantro), stalks removed

2 teaspoons ground coriander

2 teaspoons ground cumin

½ teaspoon dried chilli flakes (optional)

1 tablespoon salt flakes

½ teaspoon sweet paprika

2 cloves garlic, finely chopped

½ onion, roughly chopped

½ teaspoon bicarbonate of soda (baking soda)

750 ml (3 cups) vegetable oil

sliced tomato and tahini sauce (see page 21),
to serve

Of all the Middle Eastern dishes available today, falafel must be the most recognised – so much so that you can purchase ready-made and packet mixes. But don't ask me about making falafel from a packet – I might threaten you with your life! There is nothing that compares to freshly made falafel.

My mother has never compromised on the quality of the ingredients when she makes falafel. It's all about the chickpea. Mum uses large chickpeas (10 mm/⅓ in in size), and always finds the time to go through the chickpeas, washing them and picking out any dirt, stones or discoloured chickpeas. She uses the freshest herbs (removing most of the stalks) and minces (grinds) the mix, adding them one at a time to get a beautiful creamy green mix that remains bright and velvety when cooked (see over the page). You can eat falafel on their own, with tahini sauce or pickles, fresh vegetables, or wrapped up in bread with all of the above.

Soak the chickpeas in a large bowl of water overnight. Rinse and leave to drain for about 10 minutes.

Place the chickpeas in a food processor and process until the chickpeas resemble coarse breadcrumbs. Add the parsley, fresh and ground coriander, cumin, chilli (if using), salt, paprika, garlic and onion and process until well combined. If the mixture is too dry, add a splash of cold water to bring the ingredients together (this may not be necessary). Take care not to overprocess the mix, as it may become too wet and smooth, making it difficult to handle. It should be rough, workable and easy to shape.

Transfer the mixture to a medium bowl and fold in the bicarbonate of soda (baking soda), then chill for 30 minutes. The falafel mixture will bind together more easily once chilled.

Pour the vegetable oil into a medium heavy-based saucepan and heat to about 180°C/350°F (a cube of bread dropped in the oil will brown in 15 seconds).

Use two dessertspoons or soup spoons to shape the falafel. Working in batches of five or six at a time, shape the falafel, then very carefully lower them into the hot oil and cook for 3–4 minutes or until they are cooked through and nicely browned. Remove them with a slotted spoon and drain on kitchen paper (paper towels). (You may need to use a small sieve to remove any bits of falafel that have come away from the patties during the cooking process.) Serve immediately with sliced tomato and tahini sauce.

Note

Falafel tools, used specifically for shaping falafel, can be purchased from Middle Eastern grocers. They are not expensive, and will give your beautiful homemade falafels a professional touch.

MAKING FALAFEL

(see previous page for recipe)

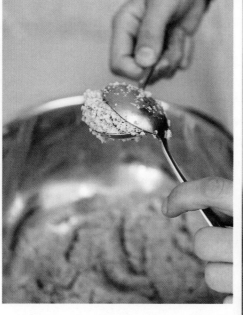

Yakhnet seafood

wa sujuk

SEAFOOD BROTH WITH SUJUK

SERVES 4

---

2 blue swimmer crabs (or can use langoustines)

4 large prawns (jumbo shrimp), shells still on, sliced

12 black mussels, scrubbed and debearded

200–300 g (7–11 oz) barramundi or sea bass fillet, skin and bones removed, cut into large pieces

2 teaspoons extra virgin olive oil

1 small brown onion, roughly diced

150 g (5 oz) sujuk, thinly sliced

small handful of mangetout (snow pea) sprouts (optional)

boiled rice, to serve (optional)

STOCK

400–500 g (14 oz – 1 lb 2 oz) raw or cooked prawn (shrimp) shells (you can pre-order these from your fishmonger) or use a whole white fish head

1 cinnamon stick

2 bay leaves

3 teaspoons ground sumac

juice of 2 limes

1 teaspoon fennel seeds

1 teaspoon cloves

2–3 teaspoons salt flakes

1 teaspoon freshly ground black pepper

This dish is fresh, warm and filling. The word 'yakhnee' is used to describe a broth made from stock that includes onions and chickpeas. I have substituted sujuk, a delicious spicy sausage, for the more usual chickpeas, to give it a bit of bite. The flavours of this stock are phenomenal; the suggestion by my seafood suppliers, Tony and Angelo, to use prawn (shrimp) shells instead of fish heads was inspired. They give the stock an amazing flavour, which is slightly nutty but not overpowering.

To make the stock, place all the ingredients in a large saucepan and cover completely with water. Cover and bring to the boil over high heat, then reduce the heat to low and simmer for 20 minutes. Remove the stock from the heat and strain through a fine-mesh sieve, discarding the solids. Reserve the stock for later.

Rinse the crabs under cold water and, using your hands, break off the legs. Pull off the main crab shell, then remove the flesh and remaining piece of bone and cut the flesh in half down the centre. Rinse off the yellow membrane under cold water and discard it.

Pour about 1 litre (4 cups) of the stock into a large saucepan and place over high heat. Add the chopped crab meat and legs, prawns (shrimp), mussels and fish. Cover and leave to steam for a few minutes.

Meanwhile, heat the olive oil in a small frying pan (skillet) over high heat, add the onion and sujuk and cook for about 5 minutes or until the onion has softened and the sujuk is starting to sweat. Pour into the pan of seafood and mix well with a large wooden spoon. Cover and cook for a further 10–15 minutes.

Serve in deep bowls with plenty of broth, garnished with a few mangetout (snow pea) sprouts (if using). This dish can be served on its own or on a bed of rice.

Hamem meshwi

BARBECUED PIGEON WITH ORANGE BLOSSOM WATER

SERVES 4

---

4 medium young pigeons (squab)

3 teaspoons salt flakes

2 teaspoons freshly ground black pepper

125 ml (½ cup) orange blossom water

5 stalks rosemary, leaves stripped

½ teaspoon sweet paprika

½ teaspoon dried chilli flakes

125 ml (½ cup) olive oil

3 maincrop or Russet potatoes, peeled and cut into 5 mm (¼ in) thick slices

100 g (3½ oz) baby spinach leaves

Young pigeons (squab) are a delicacy in Syria so it is a bit of a triumph for the males of the family to bring some home during the shooting season. I think you will like this recipe. I have added orange blossom water, traditionally used in sweets and syrups, because its subtle flavour works beautifully with the pigeon meat. Barbecuing the birds enhances the tenderness of the meat and makes this a wonderful shared plate.

Rinse the pigeons (squab) under cold water and dry thoroughly with kitchen paper (paper towels). Cut the pigeons (squab) in half along both sides of the backbone. Remove the wing tips, feet, backbone, head and neck bones and discard. Press down on the breast bone to flatten it out a little. Rub all over with 2 teaspoons salt and 1 teaspoon pepper.

In a medium bowl, mix together the orange blossom water and rosemary. Place the pigeons (squab) in the bowl and turn to coat, then cover and marinate in the fridge for about 2 hours.

Combine the paprika, chilli flakes, olive oil and remaining salt and pepper in a shallow bowl, add the potato slices and turn to coat well. Set aside.

Preheat the barbecue for about 10 minutes. Cook the potato slices on the grill for 3–4 minutes each side or until tender and lightly browned. Remove and keep warm.

Add the pigeons (squab), skin-side down, and brush lightly with the orange blossom marinade. (For a crisper skin, pat the pigeons (squab) dry with kitchen paper/paper towels before cooking.) Cook, turning from time to time, for about 5–6 minutes each side or until golden brown and slightly firm to the touch when pressed with your index finger. Transfer the pigeons (squab) to a plate, cover lightly with foil and leave to rest for 5 minutes before serving. At this point you may want to cut the pigeons (squab) in half with kitchen scissors for easier handling. If you do, you will notice that the inner flesh has a lovely rosy blush.

Spread the potato slices on a large serving plate and scatter over the baby spinach leaves. Arrange the pigeons (squab) on top and serve.

bi mazaher

LIGHTLY FRIED
WHITEBAIT

SERVES 6

---

1 kg (2¼ lb) local whitebait

2 lemons

110 g (¾ cup) plain (all-purpose) flour

3 tablespoons dried oregano

2 teaspoons seven-spice mix (see page 13)

2 teaspoons salt flakes

1 teaspoon freshly ground black pepper

180 ml (¾ cup) olive oil

Aussie toum (see page 22) or tahini sauce
(see page 21), to serve

My mother has a special way of preparing fish: she always washes it thoroughly under cold running water then places it in a bowl with layers of fresh sliced lemon. Mum believes that this removes the fishy smell and brings out the moisture in the flesh. I suggest you follow these steps for this recipe; it is particularly important when preparing whitebait to wash it thoroughly to remove any loose sand and dirt or scales.

I generally serve this with toum, but tahini sauce is a more traditional accompaniment.

Wash the whitebait in a colander under cold water to remove loose scales and sea dirt, then leave to drain for about 10 minutes. Thinly slice one of the lemons. Place the whitebait in a container, layered with the lemon slices.

In a bowl, mix together the flour, oregano, seven-spice mix, salt and pepper until well combined. Add the whitebait and toss to coat.

Heat the olive oil in a large frying pan (skillet) over high heat. Add enough whitebait to cover the base of the pan in a single layer and cook until crisp and golden, moving them around regularly so they don't stick. Make sure you move the whitebait on the edge of the pan into the centre for even cooking. Remove and drain on a plate lined with kitchen paper (paper towels). Repeat with the remaining whitebait, reheating the oil between batches.

Cut the remaining lemon into wedges. Serve with the hot whitebait and Aussie toum or tahini sauce.

bizri mekli

Scallops by lorz

ALMOND-CRUSTED SCALLOPS

SERVES 6

---

240 g (2 cups) broad (fava) bean pods

60 ml (¼ cup) lemon juice

125 ml (½ cup) olive oil

1 teaspoon salt flakes

¾ teaspoon freshly ground black pepper

80 g (½ cup) raw almonds

25 g (¼ cup) dried breadcrumbs

1 egg

1 tablespoon milk

75 g (½ cup) plain (all-purpose) flour

24 scallops, roe removed

pickled turnip, to serve

All of us at Almond Bar love our almonds, and while we don't want them to take over the menu, from time to time they do make an appearance for all the almond-lovers visiting the restaurant. In this dish, the crushed raw almonds highlight the flavour of the scallops, without being too overwhelming. Since you are serving the lightly crumbed scallops with lemony broad (fava) beans and vinegary pickled turnip you don't need to add lemon juice.

Boil the broad (fava) beans in a medium saucepan of water over medium heat until just tender but still retaining their colour. Drain and leave to cool for 5–10 minutes, then gently squeeze the beans out of the pods into a bowl. Add the lemon juice, 2 tablespoons olive oil, ½ teaspoon salt and ½ teaspoon pepper. Mix together with a large spoon, then use the back of the spoon to lightly crush the beans while they are still warm, leaving most of them intact. Cover and set aside.

Process the almonds in a food processor to a medium-fine crumb. Tip into a small bowl and stir through the breadcrumbs.

Make an egg wash by lightly whisking together the egg, milk and remaining salt and pepper.

Place the flour in a separate small bowl.

Pat the scallops dry with kitchen paper (paper towels), then dip each scallop in the flour, then the egg wash and finally in the almond crumb mixture until well coated.

Heat the remaining olive oil in a medium frying pan (skillet) over medium heat. Add about six scallops at a time and cook for 2–3 minutes each side until golden brown. Drain on kitchen paper (paper towels).

To serve, evenly drop 4 spoonfuls of the crushed broad (fava) beans on each plate and gently place a scallop on top. Serve immediately with a few pickled turnips on the side.

Shorbet jej wa riz

WARM CHICKEN & RICE SOUP

SERVES 6

---

1 × 1.4–1.6 kg (3–3½ lb) chicken

2 bay leaves

2 pieces of cassia bark or 1 cinnamon stick

2 teaspoons seven-spice mix (see page 13)

1 lemon, cut in half

2 teaspoons salt flakes

200 g (1 cup) basmati rice

2 carrots, finely diced

1 brown onion, finely chopped

2 sticks celery, finely diced

2 corn cobs, kernels cut off

small handful of flat-leaf parsley, roughly chopped

extra virgin olive oil, for drizzling

The best part about being ill in the Salloum family is Mum's chicken soup. What I love most about it is that it is so light and beautifully seasoned. The broth melts ever so slowly all the way down into your stomach, making it the perfect pick-me-up for a cloudy head.

Place the whole chicken in a large saucepan with the bay leaves, cassia or cinnamon, seven-spice mix, lemon and 1 teaspoon salt and cover the chicken completely with cold water. Cover and poach over low heat for 30–40 minutes or until cooked through.

Meanwhile, rinse the rice well, then soak in a bowl of warm water for 30 minutes. Drain.

Remove the chicken from the stock and set aside to cool for about 10 minutes. Discard the cassia or cinnamon, bay leaves and lemon halves. Add the carrot, onion, celery and corn to the stock and simmer over low heat for about 15 minutes.

Shred the chicken by hand into smallish pieces, discarding the skin and bones.

Add the shredded chicken and drained rice to the stock. Mix well and add the remaining salt, then cook, uncovered, for another 20 minutes or until the rice and vegetables are tender.

Add the parsley to the soup and cook gently for 5 minutes. Ladle into bowls and serve with a drizzle of extra virgin olive oil.

From left to right:

Standing: *cousin Issa, cousin George and his daughter Ava, Uncle Jan*

Seated: *my brother Steven, his wife Tatiana, cousin Rima and Uncle Tony*

Salads & sides

Fatoush

TOASTED BREAD SALAD

SERVES 4

---

2 cucumbers

2 tomatoes

5 radishes

½ red (bell) pepper

½ green (bell) pepper

4 iceberg lettuce leaves

large handful of purslane leaves (optional)

small handful of mint

small handful of flat-leaf parsley

3 spring onions (scallions)

1 piece Middle Eastern bread

DRESSING

3 cloves garlic, crushed

2 teaspoons salt flakes

1 teaspoon sweet paprika

3 teaspoons ground sumac

60 ml (¼ cup) extra virgin olive oil

60 ml (¼ cup) lemon juice

I once dubbed fatoush the 'Queen of salads', and I stand by that. It is one of those salads that can accompany just about any dish; you can also add poached chicken, strips of lamb or smoked salmon to make it a main meal. The key to its success is the way that the toasted bread soaks up the beautiful flavour of sumac, the wonderful citrus berry we have grown to love. When Mum used to serve fatoush as part of the dinner table, I would often start with a helping of salad before anything else touched my plate, and then continue with it as a side to other dishes.

The mysterious ingredient in this recipe that I'm often asked about is purslane, which in Arabic is known as 'baqli'. Purslane is a fleshy leaf with a slightly lemony flavour and a bitter stem (which isn't used). It is found in Middle Eastern grocers only at certain times of the year (generally in autumn and spring). If you can't find any, the salad is still very flavoursome without it.

Wash all the vegetables and herbs and allow to dry for 10 minutes.

Cut the cucumbers into quarters lengthways, then cut into 1 cm (½ in) thick slices. Cut each tomato into eight wedges, then cut each wedge in half widthways. Halve each radish and thinly slice. Remove the seeds and membrane from the peppers and cut the flesh into bite-sized cubes. Roughly pull apart the lettuce leaves and break into bite-sized pieces. Roughly chop the mint and parsley, and cut the spring onions (scallions) into 5 mm (¼ in) thick slices.

To make the dressing, place all the ingredients in a small bowl and mix together well.

Toast the Middle Eastern bread either as a whole piece or in halves under the grill or in a preheated oven at 180°C (fan)/400°F/ gas mark 6 until golden brown and crisp.

Place all the salad ingredients in a bowl, hand-crush the bread on top and pour the dressing over the salad. Toss together and serve immediately to avoid soggy bread.

Tabouli

TRADITIONAL PARSLEY, BURGHUL & TOMATO SALAD

SERVES 4–6

6 bunches flat-leaf parsley

55 g (⅓ cup) fine white burghul (bulgur wheat)

handful of mint, finely chopped

4 spring onions (scallions), root end trimmed, finely sliced

3 large tomatoes, finely diced

DRESSING

60 ml (¼ cup) lemon juice

60 ml (¼ cup) extra virgin olive oil

1 teaspoon salt flakes

½ teaspoon freshly ground black pepper

½ teaspoon sweet paprika

I know that recipes for tabouli have appeared in many cookbooks, magazines, TV shows, on the backs of cereal boxes and so on. However, like many who grew up in a Middle Eastern household, I believe there is nothing like my mum's tabouli. Has anyone I have ever come across been able to cut parsley like my mother? My cousin Rima and my father come very close, but nobody can match Mum's precision. I'm too embarrassed to serve parsley I have cut, because it could never compare. Needless to say, everyone now knows who is responsible for chopping the beautiful parsley we serve in the restaurant. Did I mention that Mum grows beds of parsley in her garden too?

This recipe is a perfect balance of ingredients. My mother created the dressing, and even though she has been making it for over forty-five years, she still tests it every time. Serve tabouli alongside barbecued meats or with seafood dishes. It is also lovely simply wrapped in lettuce leaves.

Rinse the parsley under cold water to remove any dirt, then leave it to dry for about 10 minutes. It's best to cut two bunches at a time. Remove the stalks from just under the bottom leaves. Hold the two bunches tightly together against the chopping board and, with a very sharp knife, carefully cut the parsley as finely as you can. Rinse the chopped parsley in cold water to remove any remaining dirt and fine particles, then squeeze with your hands and spread out on a clean tea (dish) towel. Leave the parsley to dry at room temperature for 20–30 minutes.

Meanwhile, place the burghul (bulgur wheat) in a small bowl with 125 ml (½ cup) water. Set aside for about 15 minutes to allow the burghul (bulgur wheat) to soak up the water and soften slightly.

To make the dressing, place all the ingredients in a small bowl and mix together well.

Place the parsley, mint, spring onion (scallion), tomato and soaked burghul (bulgur wheat) in a medium bowl. Pour the dressing over the top and toss to combine well. Serve immediately.

salatet malfouf

CABBAGE SALAD WITH ALMONDS

SERVES 4

¼ green cabbage
¼ purple cabbage
small handful of flat-leaf parsley, roughly chopped
3 radishes, thinly sliced
70 g (½ cup) flaked (slivered) almonds

DRESSING
3 cloves garlic, crushed
60 ml (¼ cup) white vinegar
60 ml (¼ cup) extra virgin olive oil
½ teaspoon salt flakes
¼ teaspoon freshly ground black pepper

Cabbage is a beautiful vegetable that has many uses in Middle Eastern cuisine. It features in soups, rolls and salads, and is sometimes even blanched and used as an edible plate for meals.

This salad is traditionally quite simple, requiring only green cabbage, a healthy amount of garlic, lemon juice, salt and olive oil. I figured it was time to fancy it up a little and give it a bit more crunch and sweetness by adding almonds, radish and red cabbage. The flavours and textures in this colourful spectacle work well alongside most dishes, but are especially good with marinated chicken (see page 124) and kafta (see page 118).

Cut the cabbage quarters in half lengthways and slice thinly across each one. Place in a large bowl and add the parsley, radish and flaked (slivered) almonds.

    To make the dressing, place all the ingredients in a small bowl and mix together well.

    Pour the dressing over the salad and gently toss together. Serve immediately.

Baladieh salad

COUNTRY CHEESE SALAD

SERVES 4

---

3 tomatoes, cut into thin wedges,
then halved widthways

200 g (7 oz) baladieh cheese, cubed

3 tablespoons chopped flat-leaf parsley

100 g (⅓ cup) canned chickpeas, drained and rinsed

50 g (⅓ cup) crushed roasted almonds

DRESSING

2 tablespoons seven-spice mix (see page 13)

1 tablespoon sugar

½ teaspoon salt flakes

60 ml (¼ cup) lemon juice

60 ml (¼ cup) olive oil

One day shortly after we opened the restaurant, I looked around my kitchen in search of the perfect ingredients to make a sweet salad dressing. I figured I wasn't using the seven-spice mix enough at that point (now I possibly overuse it!), so I combined it with some of my favourite salad ingredients and came up with the following. How can you go wrong with cheese and nuts in a salad? If you can't find baladieh cheese, use a low-salt feta instead.

Whisk together all the dressing ingredients in a small bowl, ensuring the seven-spice mix does not clump together.

Place the tomato, cheese, parsley, chickpeas and almonds in a large bowl, pour the dressing evenly over the top and gently toss to coat. Serve immediately.

salatet haloumi,

adas wa jar-jirr

HALOUMI, LENTIL & WATERCRESS SALAD

SERVES 4

1 red (bell) pepper
50 g (¼ cup) green lentils
3 large handfuls of watercress sprigs
200 g (7 oz) fresh haloumi
3 tablespoons mint leaves

DRESSING
60 ml (¼ cup) extra virgin olive oil
60 ml (¼ cup) lemon juice
1 teaspoon salt flakes (optional)
½ teaspoon freshly ground black pepper

My mother always keeps a small jar of fresh haloumi in her fridge. The twisted balls are normally eaten at breakfast time along with other beautiful dairy products, eggs and slow-cooked beans. It's funny how you realise as you grow up that not all 'breakfast' items need to be confined to breakfast. I began undoing the skeins of haloumi and serving them with salad leaves alongside meat dishes. The match was a hit and here is the light, fresh result.

Place the whole pepper under a hot grill (broiler) and cook, turning, until the skin is almost black. Remove from the grill (broiler) and allow to cool completely. Pull the skin away from the flesh and remove the stalks and seeds, then cut the flesh lengthways into 3 mm (⅛ in) wide strips.

Place the lentils in a small saucepan and cover with cold water. Bring to the boil over high heat, then reduce the heat and simmer for about 10 minutes. Test if they are ready by crushing a lentil between your fingers – it should be soft enough to press through. Drain and allow to cool.

Wash the watercress sprigs and cut off any thick stalks. Set aside to dry, or use a salad spinner for a quick dry.

Rinse the haloumi under cold water and untwist the knotted ball of cheese. The cheese may break when you do this, which is okay. Start from one end of the cheese by pulling off one strip at a time. The strips should be as thin as you can get them (2–3 mm/ ⅛ in), although you may end up with a couple of short, thicker pieces due to breakage. Continue to tear off strips until you have 200 g (½ cup).

To make the dressing, place all the ingredients in a small bowl and mix together well. Depending on how salty your haloumi is, you may not need to add the salt.

Combine the pepper, lentils, watercress, haloumi and mint leaves in a bowl and pour the dressing over the top. Gently fold together using tongs.

Salatet betinjen

AUBERGINE SALAD

SERVES 6

---

2 long, thin sweet potatoes, peeled
and cut into 5 mm (¼ in) thick slices

2 yellow or red (bell) peppers,
seeds and membrane removed, cut in half,
then cut into 12 slices

1 red onion, cut in half and thinly sliced

60 ml (¼ cup) olive oil

2 tablespoons thyme leaves

1 teaspoon salt flakes

1 teaspoon freshly ground black pepper

4 aubergines (eggplants)

large handful of flat-leaf parsley, roughly chopped

toasted Middle Eastern bread, to serve (optional)

DRESSING

1 clove garlic, crushed

60 ml (¼ cup) lemon juice

60 ml (¼ cup) extra virgin olive oil

½ teaspoon sweet paprika

2 teaspoons salt flakes

This is a modern take on Salatet el raheb (Monks' salad), which originated in Palestine and is popular all over the Levant. It is traditionally made with charred aubergine (eggplant), pomegranate molasses, onion and tomato, but I've changed the ingredients a bit to give it more texture and colour.

Preheat the oven to 200°C (fan)/425°F/gas mark 7.

Place the sweet potato, pepper and onion on a baking tray (cookie sheet), drizzle with the olive oil and sprinkle with the thyme leaves, salt and pepper. Toss lightly to coat, then roast for about 30 minutes or until the vegetables are tender. Remove and leave to cool slightly.

Meanwhile, prick each aubergine (eggplant) four or five times with a fork. Using tongs, turn the aubergines (eggplants) over an open flame until they are charred all over and the skin is starting to crack. Alternatively, you can place the aubergines (eggplants) under a hot grill (broiler) and cook until charred on all sides. Place the charred aubergines (eggplants) in a bowl of cold water to cool for about 10 minutes, then hold them under running water and remove the stalks and peel off the blackened skin. Open the aubergines (eggplants) and remove as many seeds as possible from the centre. You may not be able to take out every last seed, just do your best as this will help rid the aubergine (eggplant) of any bitterness. Once cleaned, place the aubergines (eggplants) in a colander to drain, then pull them apart by hand into larger bite-sized pieces.

To make the dressing, place all the ingredients in a small bowl and mix together well.

Combine the aubergine (eggplant), roast vegetables, parsley and dressing in a bowl and lightly toss. Serve immediately with toasted Middle Eastern bread, if liked.

Salatet smid

BURGHUL SALAD

SERVES 6

---

320 g (2 cups) coarse burghul (bulgur wheat)

¼ green cabbage, leaves separated

2 tomatoes, finely diced

large handful of flat-leaf parsley, finely chopped

70 g (¼ cup) tomato purée (paste)

3 spring onions (scallions), chopped

3 teaspoons salt flakes, or to taste

½ teaspoon dried chilli flakes

60 ml (¼ cup) extra virgin olive oil

60 ml (¼ cup) lemon juice, or to taste

10 iceberg lettuce leaves

Most young adults try to avoid having to visit their aunts and uncles during their free time. When you grow up in a Middle Eastern household, you avoid it a whole lot more because as a child it's what you had to do at least two or three times a week. However, when your aunt puts on a spread for lunch that includes this burghul (bulgur wheat) salad (which I call 'reverse tabouli' due to the increased proportion of cracked wheat to parsley), you happily visit as many times as she would like you to!

Over the years, there have been times when all the females in the family gather at my Aunt Azizi's house to have her beautiful burghul (bulgur wheat) salad. Each of us has an opinion, of course, as to how to improve it. I would want more chilli, Mum would want more lemon juice, Rima would want more salt. Carol was just happy to be eating the salad! But we all appreciated the time together and the chance to catch-up over such a simple and splendid dish.

Soak the burghul (bulgur wheat) in a bowl of cold water for about 2–3 hours. Drain and set aside.

Half-fill a medium saucepan with water and bring to the boil over high heat. Add the cabbage leaves and cook for about 3 minutes or until softened enough to fold easily. Remove from the water and leave to cool in a colander.

Combine the burghul (bulgur wheat), tomato, parsley, tomato purée (paste), spring onions (scallions), salt, chilli flakes, olive oil and lemon juice in a medium bowl. Taste and add more salt or lemon juice if needed.

Use the lettuce and cabbage leaves to scoop up the salad.

Salatet batata

POTATO SALAD

SERVES 4

---

4 maincrop or Russet potatoes, peeled and cut into 1.5 cm (⅝ in) cubes

2 tomatoes, roughly chopped

½ brown onion, thinly sliced

large handful of flat-leaf parsley, roughly chopped

small handful of mint, roughly chopped

DRESSING

1 clove garlic, crushed

1 teaspoon salt flakes

1 teaspoon sweet paprika

60 ml (¼ cup) extra virgin olive oil

60 ml (¼ cup) lemon juice

Not many people would believe me if I said it was possible to have a light, fresh potato salad, but here is the proof! My mother's potato salad is simple but well balanced. She often serves it with baked sausages (see page 52) or kafta (see page 118).

Rinse the potato cubes to remove any excess starch, then place in a medium saucepan and cover with enough cold water to come 2 cm (¾ in) above the level of the potato. Bring to the boil, then reduce the heat and simmer for 10–15 minutes or until tender, but not soft enough to fall apart. Drain and leave to cool to room temperature.

To make the dressing, place all the ingredients in a small bowl and mix together well.

Combine the potato, tomato, onion, parsley and mint in a bowl, pour over the dressing and gently toss to coat. This salad is best served while the potato is still lukewarm but it can be made ahead of time, refrigerated and served cold as well.

Loubyi bi'zeit

GREEN BEANS IN OLIVE OIL

SERVES 6

---

500 g (1 lb 2 oz) green beans, topped and tailed, then cut in half widthways

3 large ripe tomatoes

60 ml (¼ cup) extra virgin olive oil

1 large brown onion, quartered and thinly sliced

4 cloves garlic, thinly sliced

2 teaspoons salt flakes

1 teaspoon freshly ground black pepper

Whenever we take this off the menu, we get an overwhelming number of requests to bring it back. It's a very simple dish, but one that is loved by all Syrians. Some versions include a bit of seven-spice mix or cumin for additional flavour. As kids, we ate it with cubes of beef on a bed of rice – comfort food at its best.

Place the beans in a medium saucepan, cover with water and heat over medium heat until the water starts to boil. Drain and set aside.

Cut a small 'x' on the bottom of each tomato with a sharp knife. Place in a small saucepan, cover with water and cook, covered, over medium–low heat until you can see the skin peel away from the cut. Drain and then run under cold water. Peel using a small knife. Roughly chop the flesh, saving the juice and seeds for later.

Heat the olive oil in a medium saucepan over high heat, add the onion and garlic and cook for 5–6 minutes or until almost golden. Add the beans, tomato, salt and pepper and mix well.

Reduce the heat to low, then cover and cook for 25 minutes or until the beans are a dull green colour and are easy to bite through. Stir the mixture every 5–10 minutes to ensure even cooking. Serve warm or store in the refrigerator and serve cold.

Batata bi

CORIANDER POTATOES

SERVES 4

---

4 maincrop or Russet potatoes, peeled and
cut into 1–2 cm (½–¾ in) cubes

250 ml (1 cup) vegetable oil

DRESSING

large handful of coriander (cilantro), finely chopped

1 tablespoon ground coriander

2 teaspoons salt flakes

½ teaspoon freshly ground black pepper

2 cloves garlic, crushed

60 ml (¼ cup) lemon juice

60 ml (¼ cup) extra virgin olive oil

I am not the world's biggest coriander (cilantro) fan, so when I tried these I was surprised at how well the fragrant flavour of the coriander (cilantro) combined with the lemon and garlic. Now I make mini coriander- (cilantro-) potato wraps in the kitchen to snack on. I can't take the credit for that, though – Ed, one of our cooks, came up with the idea of wrapping the potatoes with some tahini sauce (see page 21), and I just decided to throw on some toum (see page 22). These days, extra helpings of potatoes are often cooked during service for good measure!

Put the potato cubes in a bowl of water to soak while you prepare the dressing.

To make the dressing, place all the ingredients in a small bowl and mix together well.

Drain the potatoes. Pour the vegetable oil into a medium heavy-based saucepan and heat over high heat to 180°C/350°F or until a small cube of bread dropped in the oil browns in 15 seconds.

You'll need to cook the potato cubes in two batches so you don't overcrowd the pan. Using a slotted spoon, carefully lower half the cubes into the oil and cover with a lid for about 2 minutes – this is to avoid small but extremely hot splatters of oil. Uncover the pan and cook for 5–6 minutes or until the potato pieces are golden and cooked through, and float to the top of the oil. Remove with a slotted spoon and drain on a large plate lined with kitchen paper (paper towels). Repeat with the remaining potato cubes.

Combine the potato cubes and dressing in a medium bowl and carefully toss with a pair of tongs until well mixed and evenly coated. These go well with just about anything but I particularly like them with hummus, baladieh salad and kafta (see pages 18, 92 and 118).

kezebra

Hindbi bi zeit

CURLY ENDIVE SAUTEED IN OLIVE OIL

SERVES 4

———————————

100 g (½ cup) dried black-eyed beans
1 bunch of curly endive
60 ml (¼ cup) extra virgin olive oil
2 small brown onions, cut in half and thinly sliced
3 cloves garlic, thinly sliced
60 ml (¼ cup) lemon juice
1 teaspoon salt flakes
½ teaspoon freshly ground black pepper
¼ teaspoon freshly grated nutmeg

———————————

I would watch Mum religiously make this dish for my father once a week as a packed lunch for work. I didn't understand why he liked it so much, considering there was no meat in it, which generally goes against my father's food beliefs! But I soon realised that my father loved picking it up with some fresh bread, a side of olives and fresh tomato and cucumber. Simple, but so delicious.

Soak the black-eyed beans in warm water for 30 minutes. Drain.

Place the beans in a small saucepan and cover with water. Bring to the boil, then reduce the heat to low and cook for 20–25 minutes or until softened. Drain.

Meanwhile, remove the roots and lower 3–4 cm (1¼–1½ in) from the curly endive. Rinse the rest of the leaves under cold water to remove any dirt, then leave to dry for about 30 minutes.

Roughly chop the endive into large bite-sized pieces.

Heat the olive oil in a large saucepan over medium heat and cook the onion and garlic until they just start to soften. Add the endive and toss to coat the leaves in the olive oil. Add the beans, lemon juice, salt, pepper and nutmeg, then reduce the heat to low and cook, covered, for 20 minutes or until the endive starts to wilt and darken in colour, stirring from time to time to stop the leaves catching on the base of the pan. Serve hot or cold.

Shish barak

MIDDLE EASTERN LAMB DUMPLINGS

SERVES 6

DUMPLINGS

300 g (2 cups) plain (all-purpose) flour

2 teaspoons salt flakes

560 ml (2¼ cups) vegetable oil

1 tablespoon olive oil

1 small brown onion, finely chopped

150 g (5 oz) minced (ground) lamb

1 teaspoon freshly ground black pepper

1 teaspoon seven-spice mix (see page 13)

60 ml (¼ cup) milk

RICE AND YOGHURT SAUCE

2 tablespoons olive oil

300 g (1½ cups) basmati rice, well rinsed

300–400 g (1¼–1⅔ cups) natural yoghurt

2 teaspoons salt flakes

1 tablespoon cornflour (cornstarch) mixed with 125 ml (½ cup) water

1 teaspoon vegetable oil

1 clove garlic, crushed

handful of mint, finely chopped

This dish is very popular in Syria, Lebanon, Jordan and Palestine. Everyone gives it a little regional twist, but this is the version I know and love. For a vegetarian variation, replace the meat filling with cooked pumpkin, spinach and corn.

To make the dough for the dumplings, place the flour, 1 teaspoon salt and 60 ml (¼ cup) of the vegetable oil in a bowl. Gradually add enough water to bring it together, then turn out onto a lightly floured surface and knead for 5 minutes or until it is soft and smooth. Cover with cling film (plastic wrap) and rest in the fridge for 30 minutes.

Meanwhile, to make the filling for the dumplings, heat the olive oil in a large frying pan (skillet) over high heat, add the onion and cook for 5 minutes or until golden. Add the meat, pepper, seven-spice mix and remaining salt and fry until the meat turns brown, breaking up any lumps with the back of a spoon. Set aside to cool.

Roll out the dough on a floured surface to a thickness of about 2 mm (1/16 in), then cut into 5 cm (2 in) squares. Place a teaspoon of filling in the centre of each square. Dip your finger into the milk and dampen the border of the dough squares with the milk. Fold the dough over to create a triangle, then gently press the edges together to seal.

Holding the dumpling from the top corner, fold the left and right corners to meet and press together to form a tortellini shape. Place on a floured surface until ready to cook.

To make the sauce, heat the olive oil in a medium saucepan over medium heat, add the rice and cook for a few minutes until it is no longer translucent. Add the yoghurt, salt and cornflour mixture and cook for 4–5 minutes, stirring to stop the rice sticking to the pan. Add about 500 ml (2 cups) water to thin out the sauce, then reduce the heat to low and cook, stirring every few minutes, for 30–40 minutes or until the rice has softened. If the sauce seems too thick, add up to another 250 ml (1 cup) water during the cooking.

Meanwhile, cook the dumplings. Heat the remaining vegetable oil in a medium heavy-based saucepan to 160°C/325°F or until a cube of bread dropped in the oil browns in 25 seconds. Add four or five dumplings at a time (it's important not to overcrowd the pan) and fry for about 5 minutes or until golden. Remove from the oil with a slotted spoon and drain on kitchen paper (paper towels). Repeat with the remaining dumplings. Cover and keep warm.

To finish the sauce, heat the vegetable oil in a small frying pan (skillet) over high heat, add the garlic and mint and cook for about 5 minutes until the garlic just starts to turn golden. Stir the garlic mixture into the yoghurt sauce, then remove from the heat.

Place the dumplings in a serving dish and pour the yoghurt sauce over the top. Leave to sit for about 5–8 minutes before serving to allow the pastry to soften slightly.

Fakhet el

ROAST LEG OF LAMB

SERVES 6

---

60 ml (¼ cup) olive oil

¼ teaspoon ground cinnamon

¼ teaspoon freshly grated nutmeg

¼ teaspoon ground cumin

¼ teaspoon sweet paprika

¼ teaspoon freshly ground black pepper

¼ teaspoon ground cardamom

8 cloves, crushed with a mortar and pestle

3 teaspoons salt flakes

1.5–2 kg (3¼–4½ lb) leg of lamb

6 cloves garlic, sliced

10 small sprigs rosemary

NUTTY RICE

2 tablespoons olive oil

40 g (¼ cup) pine nuts

35 g (¼ cup) flaked (slivered) almonds

200 g (7 oz) minced (ground) lamb

400 g (2 cups) basmati rice

1 teaspoon salt flakes

1 teaspoon freshly ground black pepper

1 teaspoon seven-spice mix (see page 13)

One of the highlights of festive celebrations at home is sitting down as a family to my mother's amazing, fall-apart, perfectly cooked lamb roast. Mum always bought two large legs of lamb; whether there were six or sixteen of us, we always ended up with a ton of leftovers. Not that I'm complaining, because it tastes even better the next day. We always have a family gathering on Christmas Eve and Easter Saturday. The location changes each year, as it is shared amongst my parents and their siblings – largely because thirty to fifty of my uncles, aunts, cousins, and their kids will be in attendance. Traditionally, Mum would par-cook the lamb the night before for about two hours or so. She would then let it cool slightly, refrigerate it overnight and then cook it for another three hours on the day. These days, she will cook it once for about three to four hours but we still get the beautiful falling-off-the-bone effect. It is always served with nutty rice, as well as hummus, baba ghanouj, tabouli (see pages 16, 18 and 90) and roasted vegetables like potato, pumpkin and brown onion.

Preheat the oven to 200°C (fan)/425°F/gas mark 7.

Mix together the olive oil, spices and salt in a bowl. Place the lamb leg on a clean surface and rub all over with the spice mix. Cut 10 small incisions in the surface of the lamb, then push the garlic and rosemary sprigs into these holes.

Place the leg in a deep baking dish and bake for 30 minutes on each side until browned. Once browned, wrap the leg in a large sheet of foil. Reduce the heat to 170°C (fan)/375°F/Gas Mark 5 and return the lamb to the oven, unwrapping it every 20–30 minutes and basting with the pan juices. Traditionally, the lamb is cooked for about 3½ hours until very tender, but if you prefer your lamb medium–rare, 1½ hours will suffice.

About half an hour before you're ready to serve, prepare the nutty rice. Heat the olive oil in a small frying pan (skillet) over medium heat and saute the pine nuts and almonds for about 2 minutes or until golden brown, stirring constantly to ensure they don't burn. Remove the nuts with a slotted spoon and drain on kitchen paper (paper towels). Pour the nutty olive oil into a large saucepan, add the meat and cook over medium heat until browned, breaking up any lumps with the back of a spoon. Add the rice, then the salt, pepper and seven-spice mix and stir to combine. Pour in enough water to cover the rice and bring to the boil, then reduce the heat and simmer, covered, for 15–20 minutes or until the rice is cooked, stirring every few minutes. When the rice is cooked, stir in the nut mixture.

When the lamb is cooked to your liking, remove it from the oven and rest, covered, in a warm place for about 15 minutes. You can either serve the nutty rice on the side or spread it over the base of a large serving dish and place the lamb leg on top.

lahm

Kousa meh-shi

STUFFED GREY COURGETTES

SERVES 4–6

---

100 g (½ cup) medium-grain rice

2 tablespoons salt flakes

16 grey courgettes (zucchini) or marrows

2 cloves garlic, crushed

2 teaspoons dried mint

200 g (7 oz) lean minced (ground) beef

1 small brown onion, finely chopped

small handful of flat-leaf parsley, roughly chopped

1 small tomato, diced

1 tablespoon seven-spice mix (see page 13)

½ teaspoon dried chilli flakes

1 teaspoon sweet paprika

½ teaspoon ground cinnamon

½ teaspoon freshly ground black pepper

60 ml (¼ cup) olive oil

2 tablespoons tomato purée (paste)

natural yoghurt and tabouli (see page 90),
to serve (optional)

Grey courgettes (zucchini) are pale in colour, with a pale white fleck, and are sometimes called 'white' courgettes (zucchini). They are shorter and chunkier than regular courgettes (zucchini), and are mainly available from speciality or Middle Eastern greengrocers. They are well suited to stuffing, usually with a beef mixture, but you can use whatever you like really. Once I decided to get really creative and replace the beef with big slices of scallop. Luckily, it went down well with the bosses (Mum and my sister). A fleshy fish like ling or cod, would work well, too.

Rinse the rice well, then soak in a bowl of warm water for about 30 minutes. Drain.

Meanwhile, place 1 tablespoon salt in a large bowl and fill the bowl to three-quarters with water. Wash and rub the skin of the courgette (zucchini) in the salted water (this will strengthen the skin for cooking). Cut the stalk and about 5 mm (¼ in) off the top of each courgette (zucchini). Discard the salty water and refill the bowl to three-quarters with fresh water. Add the garlic and dried mint and stir to combine.

Carefully hollow out the courgettes (zucchini) using a small spoon or apple corer, leaving about a 5 mm (¼ in) thick shell, and place in the bowl of minted water. This will gently infuse the mint and garlic flavour into the flesh and skin.

While the courgette (zucchini) shells are soaking, make the stuffing. Place the rice, meat, onion, parsley, tomato, seven-spice mix, chilli, paprika, cinnamon, pepper, remaining salt and 2 tablespoons olive oil in a bowl and mix together well with your hands.

Remove the courgettes (zucchini) shells from the water, shake them off and place on a dry baking tray (cookie sheet). Reserve about 500 ml (2 cups) of the mint and garlic water for cooking.

Using your hands, gently fill the courgettes (zucchini) with the stuffing, tapping the base on the bench to close up any holes. Don't overfill them as the rice will expand during cooking – leave a gap of about 5 mm (¼ in) at the top of the shells.

Pour the remaining olive oil over the base of a medium–large heavy-based saucepan. Lay the stuffed courgettes (zucchini) snugly into the pan. Stir the tomato purée (paste) into the reserved mint and garlic water and pour over the courgettes (zucchini). Place two plates on top to weight them down during cooking and cover with a lid. Bring to the boil over medium–high heat, then remove the lid, reduce the heat to low and simmer for about 40 minutes.

Carefully remove the plates and let the courgettes (zucchini) sit for about 5–10 minutes, then serve with yoghurt and a side of tabouli, if liked.

Betinjen mehshi

STUFFED SMALL AUBERGINES

SERVES 6

---

100 g (½ cup) dried chickpeas
(use split chickpeas if available)

200 g (1 cup) medium-grain rice

18 long, thin (10–15 cm/4–6 in) aubergines (eggplants)

large handful of flat-leaf parsley, finely chopped

1 small brown onion, finely chopped

1 small tomato, finely chopped and drained in a sieve

½ green (bell) pepper, seeds and membrane removed,
flesh finely chopped

½ teaspoon freshly ground black pepper

3 teaspoons salt flakes

125 ml (½ cup) olive oil

2 large tomatoes, extra, cut into 5 mm (¼ in)
thick slices

1 × 420 g (15 oz) can diced tomatoes

1 tablespoon dried mint

1 clove garlic, crushed

natural yoghurt, to serve

Note: If you're likely to make this more than
once, it's worth visiting a Middle Eastern store
and buying a manakra – a traditional tool used
to remove the flesh from aubergine (eggplant) and
courgette (zucchini).

I grew up believing that no one in our family could possibly survive as a vegetarian. Being a vegan would be something else altogether! However, over time I have come to realise that Middle Eastern cuisine in fact offers many vegetarian and vegan options. One main reason is that you can't eat meat during Lent and the other is a matter of poverty, or lack of available meat products. Although I am a meat-lover myself, I absolutely adore this dish. The aubergines (eggplants) you're looking for here are the long, thin purple ones.

Soak the chickpeas in a bowl of water overnight. Rinse and drain.

Rinse the rice well, then soak in a bowl of warm water for about 30 minutes. Drain.

Wash the aubergines (eggplants), then cut the stalk and about 2–3 cm (¾–1¼ in) off the top of each one. Carefully hollow out the aubergines (eggplants) using a small spoon or apple corer, leaving a 5 mm (¼ in) thick shell (this is a guide; it's okay if you have left a little more or less flesh around the inside of the aubergine/eggplant). Take your time so you don't break the skin.

Drain the chickpeas. If using whole chickpeas, place them on a chopping board and crush with a rolling pin to split the peas and work their skins loose. Discard the skins.

To make the stuffing, place the rice, chickpeas, parsley, onion, chopped tomato, green pepper, pepper, 1 teaspoon salt and 60 ml (¼ cup) olive oil in a bowl and mix together well.

Using your hands, gently fill the aubergine (eggplant) shells with the stuffing, tapping the base on the bench to close up any holes. Don't overfill them as the rice will expand during cooking – leave a gap of about 5 mm (¼ in) at the top of the shells.

Lay the tomato slices in the base of a large heavy-based saucepan, pour over the remaining olive oil and arrange the stuffed aubergines (eggplants) on top in neat layers.

Mix together the diced tomatoes, mint, garlic, remaining salt and 375 ml (1½ cups) water in a bowl, then pour evenly over the stuffed aubergines (eggplants).

Place two plates on top to weight the aubergines (eggplants) down during cooking and cover with a lid. Bring to the boil over medium–high heat, then remove the lid, reduce the heat to low and simmer for about 45 minutes or until the aubergines (eggplants) are very tender and the sauce is reduced. Leave to sit for a few minutes, then remove from the pan and serve with yoghurt.

Kibbeh bil

LAYERED BEEF, BURGHUL & PINE NUTS

SERVES 6

---

320 g (2 cups) fine white burghul (bulgur wheat)

700 g (1½ lb) beef kibbeh mince (ground beef kibbeh) (see recipe introduction)

2½ teaspoons salt flakes

1 tablespoon freshly ground black pepper

1 tablespoon seven-spice mix (see page 13)

small bowl of iced water

160 ml (¾ cup) olive oil

natural yoghurt, to serve

FILLING

60 ml (¼ cup) olive oil

600 g (1¼ lb) lean minced (ground) beef

3 large brown onions, finely chopped

3 teaspoons seven-spice mix (see page 13)

2 teaspoons salt flakes

1 teaspoon freshly ground black pepper

40 g (3 tablespoons) butter

80 g (½ cup) pine nuts

Kibbeh is often thought of as the national dish of Lebanon, but in fact it originates in Syria. Aleppo is said to have more than fifteen varieties of kibbeh. It is a dish that is known across the Levant, spreading as far as North Africa. I have lost count of the number of times people ask for it in the restaurant. When we eat it at home, Mum and I often squabble over the crisp edges as they are absolutely the best bit. Kibbeh mince (ground kibbeh) is usually chilled to nearly freezing point, then minced (ground) four or five times to a very fine texture. It's best to buy it from a Middle Eastern butcher if you can.

Soak the burghul (bulgur wheat) in 750 ml (3 cups) water in a large bowl for about 2 hours.

Meanwhile, to make the filling, heat 2 tablespoons olive oil in a large frying pan (skillet) over medium heat. Add the minced (ground) beef and cook until browned, breaking up any lumps with the back of a spoon. Drain any excess fat from the pan, then add the onion, seven-spice mix, salt and pepper and cook until the onion has softened. Melt the butter in a small frying pan (skillet), add the pine nuts and roast until golden brown. Stir the pine nuts and butter into the meat and onion mixture, then set aside to cool.

To make the top and bottom layers of the kibbeh, add the beef, salt, pepper and seven-spice mix to the soaked burgul (bulgur wheat). Combine the ingredients by hand, slowly pouring in about 2 tablespoons iced water to keep the mixture smooth and stop it sticking to your hands.

Preheat the oven to 200°C (fan)/425°F/gas mark 7. Generously grease a 33 × 23 × 5 cm (13 x 9 x 2 in) baking pan with olive oil.

Divide the kibbeh mixture into eight portions, and place four of them in the tin. Dampen your hands with some of the iced water, then gently flatten the kibbeh with your hands and spread it out evenly to cover the base of the pan. Spoon the filling over the top, pressing it down a little to keep the layers tight together.

Add the remaining kibbeh and gently flatten as before to create the top layer. You can also flatten the four portions into patties to make them easier to spread over the filling. Make a hole in the middle with your finger (to allow the olive oil to drip down to the lower layers) and lightly score the top layer into diamond-shaped portions. Drizzle the remaining olive oil over the top, cover the pan with foil and bake for 40–50 minutes or until nicely browned and cooked through. Rest in the pan for about 10 minutes, then cut into portions and serve with natural yoghurt.

saniyeh

Kafta

MINCED LAMB, PARSLEY & ONION SKEWERS

SERVES 6

---

1 kg (2¼ lb) minced (ground) lamb

1 brown onion, grated

large handful of flat-leaf parsley, finely chopped

1 red (bell) pepper, seeds and membrane removed, flesh grated and drained in a sieve

3 teaspoons salt flakes

½ teaspoon freshly ground black pepper

1 tablespoon seven-spice mix (see page 13)

2 tablespoons olive oil, plus extra for cooking

hummus and tabouli (see pages 18 and 90), to serve

My younger brother Steven is obsessed with kafta. When we were younger, my mother spent much of her time at family barbecues trying to get him to eat more than just kafta! Who would have thought that some minced (ground) meat, onion and parsley kneaded together with a couple of spices and barbecued would be such a beautiful combination?

Mixing minced (ground) meat with these ingredients is very Middle Eastern. There are also variations known as kofta or keftedes in Greece, Turkey and Morocco, usually shaped as meatballs. The key to good kafta is not to overcook them. You will need 20–25 bamboo skewers (approximately 20 cm/8 in long) for this recipe.

Place the lamb in a medium bowl with the onion, parsley, red (bell) pepper, salt, pepper and seven-spice mix and knead together until very well combined.

To shape the kafta mixture onto the skewers, pour the olive oil into a shallow bowl and use it to lightly coat your hands to stop the lamb sticking to them.

Hold a skewer in your left hand (if you are right-handed; vice versa if you are left-handed). Pick up a portion of kafta mixture slightly larger than a golf ball in your right hand and pierce it through the centre with the sharp end of the skewer until the ball is about 3 cm (1¼ in) from the point. Using the same hand, shape the kafta into a sausage, ensuring it remains evenly wrapped around the skewer. Leave another 3 cm (1¼ in) gap at the bottom of the skewer. You can leave more if you like, but don't make your kafta too thick otherwise they might not cook through. Repeat with the remaining mixture to make 20–25 skewers.

Preheat your barbecue for about 10 minutes and lightly oil the grill (broiler).

Cook the kafta on three sides (that is, turning twice) for 3–4 minutes each side or until browned. If you cook them on all four sides you risk overcooking the kafta, causing them to dry out. Serve immediately – *always* with hummus and tabouli. They are a team that cannot be separated!

Lahem meshwi

MARINATED LAMB SKEWERS

SERVES 4–6

---

1 kg (2¼ lb) lamb noisettes, trimmed of fat and cut into 1.5 cm (⅝ in) cubes

250 ml (1 cup) dry red wine

60 ml (¼ cup) extra virgin olive oil

½ teaspoon dried rosemary

½ teaspoon dried lemon thyme (or regular thyme)

½ teaspoon dried oregano

½ teaspoon dried marjoram

½ teaspoon dried chilli flakes

1 teaspoon seven-spice mix (see page 13)

1 teaspoon salt flakes

Middle Eastern bread, hummus (see page 18) and tabouli (see page 90), to serve

---

The general practice when cooking Middle Eastern lamb skewers is to keep it simple. In most households this normally just involves a marinade of olive oil, crushed garlic, salt and pepper. This was never good enough for Violet Salloum though. My mother has always packed the loyal lamb skewer with many flavours, and when I first started to cook meats as a young adult, I asked Mum to try red wine in the marinade. She hasn't looked back.

Many Lebanese butchers believe it is a good idea to leave some fat around the diced lamb so that when it cooks over hot coals, the meat has a smoky flavour, but of course Mum doesn't agree with that either. She insists on removing as much fat as humanly possible; even when the butcher has removed the fat, she finds more.

Lamb noisettes may be hard to find if not ordered in advance, so you can use lamb fillet instead. You'll need about 15 bamboo skewers, about 20 cm (8 in) in length, for this recipe.

Place the lamb cubes in a bowl with the wine, olive oil, herbs, spices and salt and toss well to coat. Cover and marinate in the fridge for a minimum of 2 hours, preferably overnight.

Thread about five cubes onto each skewer, leaving 2 cm (¾ in) free at the bottom and a 1 cm (½ in) gap at the top. This is essentially to make the skewers easier to handle and encourage even cooking.

Preheat the barbecue and cook the meat to your liking. For medium, cook them on three sides only for 2–3 minutes each side, depending on the strength of the heat. Test one of the pieces of lamb to see if it needs any further cooking.

Serve immediately with fresh bread, hummus and tabouli.

Jej bi tahini

CHICKEN IN TAHINI

SERVES 4–6

60 ml (¼ cup) olive oil

1 teaspoon salt flakes

1 teaspoon freshly ground black pepper

1 tablespoon ground cumin

1 clove garlic, crushed

60 ml (¼ cup) pomegranate molasses

140 g (½ cup) tahini

1 × 1.6 kg (3½ lb) chicken, cut into eight pieces

tabouli (see page 90) or fatoush (see page 88), to serve

People ask me time and time again what to do with pomegranate molasses, and what to do with leftover tahini once they have made their hummus. This chicken dish combines the two. It's a very old family recipe from my mother's side that my uncle nagged me to try. He insisted there was nothing like it. After being a little sceptical, I tried it . . . and he was maybe just a little bit right, although I haven't admitted that to him just yet! It is a very easy recipe – the flavour is all in the two super ingredients.

Place the olive oil, salt, pepper, cumin, garlic, pomegranate molasses and tahini in a large bowl and mix well to create a smooth paste. Add the chicken and coat well in the paste, then cover and refrigerate for 3–4 hours.

Preheat the oven to 190°C (fan)/400°F/gas mark 6.

Place the marinated chicken in a baking dish and bake for about 45 minutes until lightly golden. Cover and cook for a further hour until the chicken pieces are cooked through.

Serve with tabouli or fatoush.

Malfouf bi lahmet khanzeer

PORK CABBAGE ROLLS

SERVES 8

1 smallish or ½ large green cabbage
8 cloves garlic, crushed
2 teaspoon dried mint
1 teaspoon salt flakes
2 tomatoes, cut into 5 mm (¼ in) thick slices
250 ml (1 cup) lemon juice
½ teaspoon sugar (optional)
natural yoghurt, to serve

PORK STUFFING
250 g (9 oz) minced (ground) pork
small handful of flat-leaf parsley, chopped
1 small brown onion, chopped
100 g (½ cup) short-grain or medium-grain rice, rinsed and drained
1 tomato, chopped
2 teaspoons salt flakes
1 teaspoon freshly ground black pepper
½ teaspoon ground cinnamon
½ teaspoon freshly grated nutmeg

You always knew Mum was making malfouf when the smell of garlic and mint permeated the house for about two days before, during and after it was cooked. I have made a couple of changes to the traditional recipe, particularly replacing beef or lamb mince (ground beef or lamb) with pork, as I find pork gives the rolls a slight sweetness. The exact origin of this dish is unknown, but it is believed that the use of vine (grape) and cabbage leaves to wrap rice and meat dates back to ancient Egypt.

Fill a large saucepan three-quarters full with water. Place over high heat and bring to the boil.

Separate the leaves from the cabbage head. Cut away the thick stem, and cut each leaf into several triangular pieces. Dip the leaves, a few at a time, in the boiling water for 1–2 minutes until they become pliable.

To prepare the stuffing, combine all the ingredients in a bowl. Don't be concerned that the rice is raw – it will cook while the cabbage rolls are cooking. Place a good tablespoon of the stuffing on each triangular cabbage leaf, then fold in the sides and roll up from the bottom into a cigar shape.

Combine the garlic, mint and salt in a small bowl and set aside.

Lay the tomato slices over the base of a large saucepan to completely cover. Arrange the cabbage rolls on top, placing them close together so they will keep their shape. Pour in the lemon juice and 375 ml (1½ cups) water, then sit a plate face-down on top of the rolls to weight them down and help stop them unravelling during the cooking process.

Cover the pan with its lid and cook over medium–high heat for 20 minutes. Remove the lid and plate and sprinkle over the garlic and mint mixture. At this stage you can also sprinkle with the sugar, if desired – this will reduce any bitterness in the cabbage. Cover and simmer for a further 1–1½ hours until the leaves have softened completely but are not falling apart. They should now be a pale green colour.

To serve, pour out the cooking liquid, then carefully invert the pan onto a platter so the rolls tumble out gently. (Alternatively, dip your fingers in cold water and arrange the hot rolls one at a time on the platter.) Delicious served with natural yoghurt.

Jej meshwi

MARINATED CHICKEN PIECES

SERVES 6

---

1 kg (2¼ lb) mixed chicken pieces
(wings, drumsticks, breast, thighs)

3 cloves garlic, crushed

1 teaspoon salt flakes

1 teaspoon dried sage

1 teaspoon dried basil

1 teaspoon dried tarragon

1 teaspoon ground turmeric

½ teaspoon cayenne pepper

125 ml (½ cup) extra virgin olive oil,
plus extra for cooking (optional)

toum and fatoush (see pages 22 and 88),
to serve

Try Adding Some
Sumac
or
Aleppo Pepper
or
Both

As with lamb skewers (see page 120), most Middle Eastern barbecued chicken pieces are marinated in a simple combination of garlic and olive oil. When my mother prepares chicken pieces for a barbecue, however, her marinade is packed with a much greater range of ingredients, and she marinates the chicken overnight. This recipe is sure to please.

Wash the chicken pieces and pat dry with kitchen paper (paper towels).

Place the garlic, salt, herbs, spices and olive oil in a large bowl and mix together with a spoon. Add the chicken pieces and turn to coat well. Cover and leave to marinate in the fridge for at least 3 hours, preferably overnight.

The best way to cook the chicken is on a barbecue. However, you can also bake it in a preheated 190°C (fan)/400°F/gas mark 6 oven for about 45 minutes, turning once.

If using a barbecue, preheat it well on a high setting. Lightly coat the grill with some olive oil to avoid sticking, then add the chicken pieces and cook on all sides until browned and cooked through. This should take 7–8 minutes, depending on the heat of your barbecue. Serve immediately with toum and fatoush.

Note
This marinade also works well with large cubes of chicken breast fillet threaded onto skewers.

Yakhnet batata wa kafta

KAFTA & POTATO STEW

SERVES 6

---

400 g (2 cups) basmati rice

1 quantity kafta mixture (see page 118)

125 ml (½ cup) olive oil

1 brown onion, roughly chopped

4 cloves garlic, thinly sliced

3 large potatoes, peeled
and cut into 1.5 cm (⅝ in) cubes

3 large ripe tomatoes, roughly chopped

2 tablespoons tomato purée (paste)

1 piece of cassia bark or 1 cinnamon stick

2 bay leaves

1 teaspoon freshly ground black pepper

2 teaspoons salt flakes

The aroma wafting down the driveway as I came home from school would immediately alert me that Mum was making something with kafta and potatoes. That wonderful aroma, plus the clunking of wooden spoons against my mother's beloved Bessemer pots, would have me running into the kitchen, eager with anticipation. This comforting stew is a perfect winter warmer.

Rinse the rice well, then soak in a bowl of warm water for about 30 minutes.

Meanwhile, form the kafta mixture into 2–3 cm (¾–1¼ in) meatballs.

Heat 60 ml (¼ cup) of the olive oil in a medium heavy-based saucepan over medium–high heat, add the onion and garlic and cook until softened. Add the potato and saute for about 8 minutes or until golden.

Reduce the heat to medium–low and add the kafta balls. Cook for about 10 minutes or until they begin to brown. Stir in the chopped tomato, tomato purée (paste), cassia or cinnamon, bay leaves, pepper and 1 teaspoon salt. Add 250 ml (1 cup) water to create a sauce, then cover and leave to simmer for 30–35 minutes.

Drain the rice well in a sieve. Heat the remaining olive oil in a medium saucepan over high heat for about 3 minutes, add the rice and stir to coat generously with the hot oil. Add 1 litre (4 cups) water and the remaining salt, then reduce the heat to low and cook, covered, for 15 minutes or until the rice is tender and has absorbed all the liquid. Stir just once or twice during this time.

Spoon the rice onto a serving plate and spread it out evenly. Top with the kafta and potato stew and serve with your choice of crisp, fresh vegetables, such as cucumber, radish and watercress, and some olives.

Mouzet el kharoof

STUFFED BONELESS LAMB SHANKS

SERVES 6

---

150 g (5 oz) freekeh

1 granny smith apple, cored, peeled and grated

1 teaspoon ground cinnamon

1 tablespoon sugar

2 teaspoons salt flakes

6 boneless lamb shanks

2 very ripe tomatoes, roughly chopped

250 ml (1 cup) dry red wine

1 tablespoon seven-spice mix (see page 13)

I came across this beautiful cut of lamb when I was working as a guide on a food tour through Sydney. I'd never seen it before so I was eager to give it a try. I combined it with some granny smith apples, cinnamon, tomato, sugar and a dry red, giving it the rich, sweet–sour flavours I love so much. The freekeh absorbs all the flavours effortlessly, and the texture of the lamb is superb, especially reheated the next day! It is certainly a very unconventional dish, because in Middle Eastern cuisine we rarely combine sweet flavours with savoury ones. Not even my mother could understand how I could put these ingredients together, but once she had a taste, she was won over.

Preheat the oven to 190°C (fan)/400°F/gas mark 6.

Wash the freekeh in a bowl of warm water (this is to flush out any burnt wheat particles that need to be discarded). Drain and wash again in the same way, then leave it in a sieve to drain.

Combine the freekeh, apple, cinnamon, sugar and 1 teaspoon salt in a bowl and mix together well.

Lay the shanks on a clean surface with the inside layer of the shanks facing up (the outer layer will have a thin membrane covering it and the inside will have more texture and sinews through the meat). Score through the meatiest part of the lamb to make a small incision, enough to fit 2–3 teaspoons of the freekeh stuffing. Spoon in the stuffing and press it down, then roll the shank around to enclose it.

For each shank, cut a 30 cm (12 in) length of kitchen string (twine). Wrap the string (twine) around one end of the shank and tie a knot (leaving about 2 cm/¾ in excess string/twine), then wrap the string (twine) around the shank two or three times until it reaches the other end. Pull the string (twine) back to the knot end and tie the ends together as tightly as possible. The shank will resemble a mini deboned lamb roast. Place all the shanks in a roasting pan.

Place the tomato, wine, seven-spice mix and remaining salt in a small bowl and mix together well, pressing down lightly against the tomato with the back of a spoon. Pour over the lamb shanks, then cover the pan with foil and bake for 2 hours. Reduce the heat to 150°C (fan)/325°F/gas mark 3, then turn the shanks over and cook, covered, for another 3 hours until the lamb is beautiful and tender. I love to serve these with aubergine (eggplant) salad (see page 96) or curly endive sauteed in olive oil (see page 105).

samki harra

CHILLI FISH

---

4 × 200–300 g (7–11 oz) barramundi or sea bass
fillets, bones removed

1 tomato, finely diced

25 g (¼ cup) walnuts

flat-leaf parsley sprigs, to garnish

1 lemon, cut into wedges (optional)

MARINADE

1 clove garlic, peeled and left whole

3 tablespoons chopped coriander (cilantro)

2 teaspoons ground coriander

½ teaspoon dried chilli flakes

2 teaspoons salt flakes

280 g (1 cup) tahini

250 ml (1 cup) lemon juice

50 g (½ cup) walnuts

Although most Middle Eastern food is not hot, some dishes do have a bit of a bite to them. One of these is samki harra, which is said to have originally come from Tripoli, in northern Lebanon. It is popular in quite a few Middle Eastern countries, each of which has of course made changes to the recipe. This is what I like to think of as the Australian/Syrian version.

To make the marinade, place the garlic, fresh and ground coriander, chilli and salt in a food processor and blend until the garlic is finely chopped and the ingredients are well combined. Add the tahini and lemon juice. If the tahini pulls together and stiffens, add 125–180 ml (½–¾ cup) water to loosen the mix and give it a thick sauce consistency. How much water you need will depend on the amount of oil in the tahini you are using. Finally, add the walnuts and pulse briefly so they are still in larger pieces.

Pour the marinade into a shallow non-metallic dish, add the fish fillets and turn to coat well. Cover and marinate in the fridge for at least 2 hours, but no more than 4 hours otherwise the fish will start to 'cook' in the marinade.

Preheat the oven to 200°C (fan)/425°F/gas mark 7.

Line a deep baking dish large enough to fit all four fillets with baking paper. Place the fillets in the dish in a single layer and pour the marinade evenly over the top. It is okay if the fillets are snugly nestled against one another.

Bake for 20–25 minutes or until cooked through. To check the fish, insert a fork in the thickest part of the flesh and if the fork goes through easily it is ready.

Sprinkle the diced tomato over a serving plate and arrange the fish fillets on top. Hand-crush the walnuts over the fish. Finish with a few sprigs of parsley and serve with lemon wedges, if liked.

Bamyi

bi lahmi

SAUTEED OKRA
& LAMB

SERVES 4

---

400 g (14 oz) okra (ladies fingers)

60 ml (¼ cup) extra virgin olive oil

2 cloves garlic, thinly sliced

2 brown onions, roughly chopped

600 g (1¼ lb) lamb fillet, loin or backstrap, trimmed
and cut into 1.5 cm (⅝ in) cubes

4 ripe tomatoes, roughly chopped

1 red (bell) pepper, seeds and membrane removed,
flesh finely chopped

2–3 teaspoons salt flakes

1 teaspoon freshly ground black pepper

½ teaspoon freshly grated nutmeg

½ teaspoon ground cinnamon

small handful of flat-leaf parsley, roughly chopped

mashed potato or boiled rice, to serve

Okra (ladies fingers) is a member of the squash family, and is usually cooked as part of a stew. I grew up eating okra (ladies fingers) regularly; at times it was sauteed with onions and garlic and served with fresh bread, but I think the best way to eat it is like this – in a tomato stew with beautifully cooked lamb, spooned over fluffy mashed potato.

Rinse the okra (ladies fingers) under cold water and rub with your fingers. Cut off the small tip at the top of each okra (ladies fingers), then leave to dry on a tea (dish) towel for about 30 minutes.

Heat the olive oil in a large heavy-based saucepan over high heat, add the garlic and onion and cook until softened. Reduce the heat to medium. Add the lamb and stir to coat in the oil mixture, then cook for 8–10 minutes or until browned. Remove the lamb from the pan. Add the okra (ladies fingers) and cook for 5–7 minutes or until they are soft and spongy when pressed gently with a spoon.

Return the lamb to the pan, and stir in the tomato, red (bell) pepper, salt, pepper, nutmeg and cinnamon. Cover and cook over low heat for about 20–25 minutes. Add the parsley and cook for a further 10 minutes, then remove from the heat and leave to sit for 5 minutes.

Serve on creamy mashed potato or a bed of boiled rice.

Mukloubi

UPSIDE-DOWN LAMB & RICE DISH

SERVES 6-8

600–700 g (1¼–1½ lb) aubergines (eggplants), peeled and cut into 5 mm (¼ in) thick slices

2 tablespoons salt flakes

1 kg (2¼ lb) lamb noisettes or lamb loin or backstrap, trimmed of fat and cut into 2 cm (¾ in) cubes

50 g (¼ cup) seven-spice mix (see page 13)

½ lemon

2 pieces of cassia bark or 1 cinnamon stick

3 bay leaves

250 ml (1 cup) vegetable oil

60 g (4 tablespoons) butter

500 g (2½ cups) basmati rice

80 g (½ cup) pine nuts

extra virgin olive oil, for drizzling

natural yoghurt, to serve

This was my favourite dish when I was growing up. It is absolutely amazing, and combines all the things I love: rice, lamb, fried aubergine (eggplant) for a smoky flavour and nuts for crunch. Not to mention the yoghurt I drown it in as well. I never have just one serving; it must be two, even if it means not being able to move for the rest of the day.

The first time I ever had this dish was in Syria when I was eight years old, and my beautiful grandmother Melia turned it out onto a large round platter and called us to the table. Just like the old days, she asked us all to sit around the platter, grab a spoon and eat until we couldn't move. So we did.

Place the aubergine (eggplant) slices in a bowl and cover with cold water and 1 tablespoon salt. Leave to soak for 30 minutes, then remove and lay flat on a clean tea (dish) towel to dry on both sides. This will take about 1½–2 hours.

Meanwhile, place the lamb in a medium saucepan and cover with water. Add the seven-spice mix, lemon, cassia bark or cinnamon, bay leaves and remaining salt. Bring to the boil, then reduce the heat to low and cook, covered, for about 2 hours or until the lamb is tender.

Heat the vegetable oil in a deep frying pan (skillet). Add the aubergine (eggplant) in batches and cook on both sides until brown. Remove and drain on a plate lined with kitchen paper (paper towels). Continue stacking the cooked aubergine (eggplant) on the plate, with additional kitchen paper (paper towels) between each layer to soak up any excess oil.

Melt 40 g (3 tablespoons) of the butter in a medium saucepan, add the rice and stir until the rice is well coated in the butter.

Remove the lamb from the saucepan, reserving the stock, and arrange in the base of a large flameproof casserole dish. Spoon over half the rice, top with the cooked aubergine (eggplant) and finally the remaining rice. Strain the lamb stock, and pour evenly over the rice – add enough stock to just cover the rice.

Cover with a lid and cook over low heat for 40 minutes or until the rice is fluffed up and cooked through.

While the rice is cooking, melt the remaining butter in a small frying pan (skillet), add the pine nuts and cook over medium heat until the pine nuts are golden brown, stirring regularly so they don't catch and burn. Remove with a slotted spoon and drain on kitchen paper (paper towels).

Once the rice is cooked, take a large plate that fits securely around the perimeter of the casserole dish the mukloubi has been cooking in. Set the plate over the casserole, upside-down, then carefully invert the mukloubi onto the plate. Lift off the casserole dish.

Scatter the pine nuts over the mukloubi and drizzle with a little extra virgin olive oil. Serve with plenty of natural yoghurt.

bi lahmi

Ablama

STUFFED AUBERGINE COOKED IN A YOGHURT SAUCE

SERVES 6

---

12 long, thin aubergines (eggplants), 10–15 cm (4–6 in) long, stems and about 5 mm (¼ in) of flesh removed

180 ml (¾ cup) olive oil

1 small brown onion, finely chopped

3 cloves garlic, crushed

200 g (7 oz) minced (ground) beef

50 g (¼ cup) short-grain rice, rinsed well and drained

2 teaspoons salt flakes

½ teaspoon freshly ground black pepper

½ teaspoon seven-spice mix (see page 13)

¼ teaspoon ground cinnamon

1 teaspoon dried oregano

80 g (½ cup) pine nuts

YOGHURT SAUCE

2 eggs, beaten

420 g (1½ cups) natural yoghurt

40 g (3 tablespoons) butter

2 cloves garlic, crushed

1 teaspoon salt flakes

2 tablespoons dried mint

This is an extremely popular dish in Syria. Once again, there are a few versions, depending on where it is made, but this is the one I grew up with. It's a very satisfying meal, perfect for a cold night in. I like to serve it with a decent amount of yoghurt sauce, which is soaked up by the rice filling, creating beautiful juices on the plate at the end of the meal to be mopped up with bread or just eaten as a warm yoghurt soup.

Core the aubergines (eggplants) with a thin, sharp knife, apple corer or, better yet, with an aubergine (eggplant) corer (found in Middle Eastern stores), making sure you don't break the skins.

Heat 125 ml (½ cup) olive oil in a large frying pan (skillet) over medium heat and saute the aubergines (eggplants), turning often, until they are cooked on all sides. Remove and place in a colander or on kitchen paper (paper towels) to drain and cool.

To the same oil, add the onion and garlic and cook over medium heat for about 5 minutes. Stir in the meat, rice, salt, pepper, seven-spice mix, cinnamon and oregano and cook until the meat is browned, breaking up any lumps with the back of a spoon. Remove from the heat and allow to cool.

Preheat the oven to 160°C (fan)/350°F/gas mark 4.

Meanwhile, heat the remaining olive oil in another frying pan (skillet), add the pine nuts and cook over medium heat until they turn golden brown. Remove with a slotted spoon and drain on a couple of layers of kitchen paper (paper towels). Stir into the cooled beef mixture.

Spoon the beef stuffing into the aubergines (eggplants) almost to the top (about 5 mm/¼ in away) and set aside.

To prepare the yoghurt sauce, combine the eggs and yoghurt in a large deep saucepan and stir until well blended. Add 750 ml (3 cups) cold water and stir well. Place over medium heat and stir gently with a wooden spoon until the mixture comes to the boil, then reduce the heat to low so it doesn't curdle or separate.

Melt the butter in a small saucepan over medium heat, then add the garlic, salt and mint and cook until the garlic turns golden brown. Stir the garlic mixture into the yoghurt sauce until well combined.

Place the aubergines (eggplants) in a single layer in a medium baking dish and pour the yoghurt sauce evenly over the top. Bake for 1 hour, then serve hot.

Sheikh el mehshi

STUFFED BABY AUBERGINES

SERVES 4

---

180 ml (¾ cup) olive oil

12 small aubergines (eggplants), stalks trimmed

40 g (¼ cup) pine nuts

1 small brown onion, finely chopped

200 g (7 oz) minced (ground) lamb

½ teaspoon ground allspice or pimento

¼ teaspoon ground cinnamon

salt flakes and freshly ground black pepper

4 ripe tomatoes, roughly chopped

This ancient dish is said to date back to the Ottoman Empire. The first time my mother made it, we all wondered why the rice was served separately instead of being inside the aubergines (eggplants), but we soon got the hang of it. The simple tomato sauce and the way you break the melting aubergines (eggplants) onto the rice make this a taste sensation. For this recipe, use small purple aubergines (eggplants), about 5–7 cm (2–2¾ in) long.

Preheat the oven to 200°C (fan)/425°F/gas mark 7.

Heat 125 ml (½ cup) olive oil in a medium frying pan (skillet) over medium–high heat. Add the whole aubergines (eggplants), in batches of four to six at a time, and cook until lightly browned and soft. Remove with a slotted spoon and rest on a flat plate lined with kitchen paper (paper towels). Allow to cool.

Discard the oil from the frying pan (skillet) and wipe clean. Add the remaining olive oil and heat over medium–high heat. Add the pine nuts and cook, stirring constantly, until golden. Remove with a slotted spoon and drain on kitchen paper (paper towels). Add the onion and saute until soft and translucent, then add the meat and cook until browned, breaking up any lumps with the back of a spoon. Sprinkle the allspice or pimento, cinnamon, salt and pepper over the meat and onion and saute for about 5 minutes. Return the pine nuts to the pan and mix through, then remove from the heat.

Make a deep slit almost halfway through the side of each aubergine (eggplant). Using a small spoon, fill the soft flesh with the meat mixture, then place the aubergines (eggplants) in a deep baking dish, snugly lined up beside one another. Reserve any remaining meat mixture.

Make a quick sauce by combining the tomato, salt, pepper and 250 ml (1 cup) water in a bowl. Stir in any reserved meat mixture.

Pour the tomato sauce over the stuffed aubergines (eggplants) and bake for about 30 minutes or until the aubergines (eggplants) have softened. Serve immediately. This is delicious served with rice with fried vermicelli (see page 159).

Fat-tet lahmi

LAYERED LAMB & CRUSHED BREAD

SERVES 4

---

1 teaspoon bicarbonate of soda (baking soda)
200 g (1 cup) dried chickpeas
20 g (1½ tablespoons) butter
40 g (¼ cup) pine nuts
250 g (9 oz) minced (ground) lamb
½ teaspoon ground cinnamon
½ teaspoon ground cumin
2 teaspoons salt flakes
¼ teaspoon freshly ground black pepper
280 g (1 cup) natural yoghurt
1 tablespoon extra virgin olive oil
pickled vegetables or hard-boiled eggs, to serve

TAHINI SAUCE
280 g (1 cup) tahini
60 ml (¼ cup) lemon juice
½ teaspoon salt flakes
2 cloves garlic, crushed

FRIED BREAD
125 ml (½ cup) olive oil
3 pieces Middles Eastern bread, cut into eighths

The beauty of fatteh, meaning 'crushed', is that it is a simple meal and there are enough variations to suit everyone's tastes. You can make it with chicken or lamb, or as a vegetarian dish. A great mixture of complementary flavours and textures, it's a guaranteed hunger-buster. It is particularly popular in Damascus, where you can find fatteh sellers with their carts at any time of the day. However, traditionally it is a breakfast dish. You will need to soak the chickpeas overnight so start this recipe a day ahead.

Dissolve the bicarbonate of soda (baking soda) in a large bowl of water, add the chickpeas and soak overnight. Rinse and drain.

Place the chickpeas in a medium saucepan and cover them with about 2 litres (8 cups) water. Bring to the boil over high heat, skimming off the foam that forms on the surface, then reduce the heat to low, cover and simmer for 40–50 minutes or until the chickpeas can be easily crushed between two fingers. Take off the heat and leave in the hot water until ready to use.

Melt the butter in a medium frying pan (skillet) over medium heat and fry the pine nuts until they are golden brown, stirring regularly. Remove from the pan with a slotted spoon and drain well on kitchen paper (paper towels).

Add the meat, cinnamon, cumin, salt and pepper to the same pan and cook until the lamb is nicely browned, breaking up any lumps with the back of a spoon. Turn off the heat and leave the meat in the pan.

To make the tahini sauce, place all the ingredients in a food processor, add 60 ml (¼ cup) water and process until smooth and well combined.

For the fried bread, heat the olive oil in a deep frying pan (skillet), add the bread in batches and fry until crisp and golden. Remove and drain on kitchen paper (paper towels). You can also toast or grill (broil) the bread, but if you do this you must serve the dish immediately as the bread will quickly become soggy.

To assemble the fatteh, place the bread at the bottom of a large serving bowl, crushing it lightly by hand (don't crush into small pieces – keep them a substantial size). Remove the cooked chickpeas from the pan with a slotted spoon and scatter over the bread. Spoon on the lamb mixture, then pour the tahini sauce over the top, followed by the yoghurt and pine nuts. Finish with a drizzle of extra virgin olive oil and serve with pickled vegetables or hard-boiled eggs.

Freekeh bi jej

FREEKEH WITH CHICKEN & ROASTED NUTS

SERVES 6

---

1 × 1.2–1.6 kg (2¾–3½ lb) chicken

50 g (¼ cup) seven-spice mix (see page 13)

2 pieces of cassia bark or 1 cinnamon stick

1 stick celery

1 carrot

1 small lemon, cut in half

2 bay leaves

2 tablespoons salt flakes

3 small brown onions

450 g (3 cups) freekeh

130 g (½ cup) butter

3 ripe tomatoes, roughly chopped

3 grey or green courgettes (zucchini) or marrows, cut in half lengthways and cut into 5 mm (¼ in) thick slices

80 g (½ cup) blanched almonds

40 g (¼ cup) pine nuts

Every so often I visit my friends at Harkola, a supplier of Middle Eastern products, to see if I can discover any new ingredients. A few years back, I rediscovered freekeh, which is made from roasted unripe wheat grains, and is a good alternative to rice or potatoes. Freekeh originated in Syria, and my aunty used to make it for us when we were kids. I picked some up and decided to try the dish that my Aunty Najet had made 21 years ago. I hope you like the result as much as I do.

Place the whole chicken in a large saucepan and cover with cold water. Add the seven-spice mix, cassia or cinnamon, celery, carrot, lemon, bay leaves and 1 tablespoon salt. Cut one of the onions in half and add to the pan, then cover and cook over medium heat for 30 minutes, skimming off any foam from the surface. Reduce the heat to low and simmer gently, covered, for a further 30 minutes or until the chicken is cooked through.

Remove the chicken from the pan and allow to cool slightly, then remove the skin and bones, trying to leave the meat intact as much as possible. Strain the stock through a sieve and reserve to cook the freekeh, discarding the solids.

Wash the freekeh in warm water to flush out any burnt grains. Drain and set aside.

Roughly chop the two remaining onions. Melt about 80 g (⅓ cup) of the butter in a medium saucepan, add the onion and cook over medium heat until softened slightly. Add the tomato, courgettes (zucchini) and remaining salt and cook for another 3 minutes. Stir in the freekeh until well coated with the butter mixture.

Slowly pour in 1.5 litres (6⅓ cups) of the reserved stock and bring to the boil over medium heat. Reduce the heat to low and cook, covered, for 25–30 minutes, stirring every 10 minutes or so to separate the grains. Just before the freekeh has soaked up all the stock, give it a final stir and add the chicken pieces. Cover and cook for 10–15 minutes over low heat – the freekeh should still be a little moist.

While the chicken is warming in the freekeh, melt the remaining butter in a medium frying pan (skillet). Add the almonds and pine nuts and fry until lightly golden. Do not drain the nuts on kitchen paper (paper towels) as you will need the excess butter.

Transfer the freekeh and chicken to a large serving plate and pour the fried nuts and butter over the top. Serve immediately.

Fat-tet jej

LAYERED CHICKEN WITH MIDDLE EASTERN BREAD, SPICED BEEF RICE & TAHINI YOGHURT SAUCE

SERVES 4–6

---

1 × 1.2–1.5 kg (2¾–3¼ lb) chicken

1 small onion, roughly chopped

1 piece of cassia bark or 1 cinnamon stick

½ lemon

2 teaspoons seven-spice mix (see page 13)

1 teaspoon salt flakes

2 pieces Middle Eastern bread

80 g (½ cup) roasted unsalted cashews

small handful of flat-leaf parsley, roughly chopped (optional)

SPICED BEEF RICE

2 tablespoons olive oil

300 g (11 oz) minced (ground) beef

½ teaspoon ground cinnamon

½ teaspoon freshly ground black pepper

½ teaspoon sweet paprika

300 g (1½ cups) basmati rice

TAHINI YOGHURT SAUCE

560 g (2 cups) natural yoghurt

2 cloves garlic, crushed

70 g (¼ cup) tahini

Another dish that originated in Damascus, the robust flavours, combination of textures and satisfaction that come with every layer make this a wonderful meal to share. The bread soaks up the flavours in the fatteh and the fragrant chicken stock.

Place the chicken, onion, cassia or cinnamon, lemon, seven-spice mix and salt in a large saucepan or stockpot. Add enough cold water to completely cover the chicken and bring to the boil over high heat, skimming off any foam as it appears, then reduce the heat to low and simmer for 50 minutes or until the chicken is cooked through.

Lift the chicken out of the stock and leave to cool for about 15 minutes. Remove the skin and bones. Strain the stock, discarding the solids, and reserve the stock for later.

Meanwhile, toast the bread under a grill (broiler) until golden brown and crisp. You could also do this in a 200°C (fan)/425°F/gas mark 7 oven. Break the bread into small pieces and place in a large, deep serving dish.

To make the spiced beef rice, heat the olive oil in a large saucepan over medium heat, add the beef, cinnamon, pepper and paprika and cook until the meat is browned, breaking up any lumps with the back of a spoon. Stir in the rice, then add 750 ml (3 cups) of the reserved stock and simmer, covered, for 15–20 minutes or until the rice is cooked.

For the tahini yoghurt sauce, place all the ingredients in a small bowl and mix well.

Shortly before you want to eat, pour 125 ml (½ cup) of the reserved stock over the toasted bread in the serving dish. Spoon the beef and rice mixture over the bread and top with the yoghurt sauce. Scatter the chicken pieces over the top and garnish with the cashews and parsley (if using). Serve immediately.

Kibbeh

bi kishk

STUFFED LAMB SHELLS IN YOGHURT & WHEAT SOUP

SERVES 4-6

---

180 ml (¾ cup) olive oil

1 small brown onion, finely chopped

100 g (3½ oz) minced (ground) lamb

1 teaspoon seven-spice mix (see page 13)

1 teaspoon salt flakes

50 g (⅓ cup) pine nuts

roughly chopped flat-leaf parsley, to garnish

KIBBEH SHELL

75 g (⅓ cup) fine white burghul (bulgur wheat)

½ brown onion, grated

½ red (bell) pepper, seeds and membrane removed, flesh grated

1 teaspoon salt flakes

½ teaspoon freshly ground black pepper

½ teaspoon seven-spice mix (see page 13)

½ teaspoon dried mint

200 g (7 oz) lamb kibbeh mince (ground kibbeh) (see page 116)

250 ml (1 cup) iced water

KISHK

60 ml (¼ cup) olive oil

1 brown onion, roughly chopped

8 cloves garlic, crushed

200 g (2 cups) kishk powder

1 teaspoon salt flakes

½ teaspoon freshly ground black pepper

I hadn't had this dish in years until one day a few months ago, when my cousin Rima invited my sister, my mother and me to her house for lunch. This is what she had made for us. Rima is an unbelievable cook, so naturally it was incredible.

Heat 60 ml (¼ cup) olive oil in a medium saucepan, add the onion and cook over medium heat until lightly golden. Add the meat, seven-spice mix and salt and cook until the meat is nicely browned, breaking up any lumps with the back of a spoon. Turn off the heat. Heat the remaining olive oil in a small frying pan (skillet) and roast the pine nuts until browned. Remove with a slotted spoon and mix into the lamb stuffing. Set aside.

To make the kibbeh shell, soak the burghul (bulgur wheat) in 250 ml (1 cup) water in a large bowl for about 10-15 minutes. Squeeze out any excess liquid from the onion and red (bell) pepper, then place in a bowl. Add the salt, pepper, seven-spice mix, mint and kibbeh meat and gently knead together by hand. As you knead, pour in a splash of iced water two or three times to help bring the ingredients together and give the shell mixture a smooth, shiny finish. Reserve the remaining iced water for shaping the kibbeh. Refrigerate the kibbeh mix for half an hour or so.

To assemble the kibbeh, roll the shell mixture into balls slightly smaller than a golf ball, then use your index finger to create a small indent in the centre of each ball. Fill each indent with a teaspoon of the lamb stuffing mixture, then gently press together and roll back into a ball shape. Keep the reserved iced water handy to lightly coat your hands so the shell mixture doesn't stick to your fingers.

Heat the remaining olive oil in a large frying pan (skillet) over medium heat and cook the kibbeh in batches for 3-5 minutes or until browned and cooked through. Remove and drain on kitchen paper (paper towels).

To prepare the kishk, heat the olive oil in a large saucepan over medium heat, add the onion and garlic and cook for 5 minutes or until golden. Add the kishk powder, salt and pepper and cook, stirring constantly, for another 3-4 minutes or until aromatic. Gradually add 1.5 litres (6⅓ cups) water, stirring until the kishk starts to boil and thicken, then reduce the heat to low and cook for another 15 minutes, stirring occasionally.

Add the kibbeh to the kishk and and mix together well. Spoon into shallow bowls and finish with a sprinkling of parsley.

Burghul bi lahmi

CRACKED WHEAT & BEEF STEW

SERVES 6

---

1 teaspoon bicarbonate of soda (baking soda)

200 g (1 cup) dried large chickpeas

1 kg (2¼ lb) beef rump, cut into 1.5 cm (⅝ in) cubes

1 piece of cassia bark or 1 cinnamon stick

2 bay leaves

480 g (3 cups) coarse white burghul (bulgur wheat)

2 tablespoons olive oil

3 brown onions, diced

2 teaspoon salt flakes

1 teaspoon freshly ground black pepper

1 tablespoon seven-spice mix (see page 13)

natural yoghurt, to serve

Many people are at a loss as to how to use burghul (bulgur wheat), a lighter alternative to rice. This is the perfect dish for it. The beauty of it is that it takes on the flavour of the stock so well. It is much loved in the Salloum household and my mother has been making it for as long as I can remember. The chickpeas need to soak overnight so start this recipe a day ahead.

Dissolve the bicarbonate of soda (baking soda) in a large bowl of water, add the chickpeas and soak overnight. Rinse and drain.

Bring a medium saucepan of water to the boil, add the chickpeas and return to a simmer. Cook for about 40 minutes or until the chickpeas are tender and can be crushed between two fingers. Drain and allow to cool.

Meanwhile, place the beef cubes in a large saucepan, along with the cassia or cinnamon and bay leaves. Cover with water and bring to the boil, then reduce the heat to low and cook, covered, for about 30 minutes or until cooked. Drain, discarding the cassia or cinnamon and bay leaves, but reserve the stock for later.

Rinse the burghul (bulgur wheat) two or three times in warm water, then drain in a sieve.

Heat the olive oil in a large saucepan over medium heat, add the onion and cook for 5 minutes or until golden brown. Add the beef cubes, chickpeas and then the burghul (bulgur wheat). Sprinkle over the salt, pepper and seven-spice mix and pour in about 2 litres (8 cups) of the reserved stock. Mix everything together and bring to the boil, then reduce the heat to low and cook, covered, for 40 minutes or until the burghul (bulgur wheat) is tender and has soaked up all the stock, stirring every few minutes.

Stir through a dollop of yoghurt just before serving.

Macaroni bi laban

SPAGHETTI WITH YOGHURT

SERVES 4

---

500 g (1 lb 2 oz) spaghetti

560 g (2 cups) natural yoghurt

2 teaspoons dried mint

1 teaspoon salt flakes

3 cloves garlic, crushed

Very occasionally my mother would allow us to have an alternative meal at dinner if we weren't up to eating what she had prepared. One day, my mother had made her version of spaghetti bolognese (not very Middle Eastern I know; it was one of the dishes Mum would make on a 'lazy day'). My sister Carol didn't feel like the bolognese sauce but was happy to have the spaghetti on its own. My mother would not hear of it! She came up with her own version of a traditional dish, spaghetti with yoghurt, and it has been one of her best quick stand-by meals ever since. Both the Syrians and Lebanese eat this – some people omit the mint, while others prefer to cook the yoghurt slightly for a warmer meal. Mum adds garlic, for something a bit different.

Cook the spaghetti in salted boiling water until al dente, following the packet instructions.

While the spaghetti is cooking, place the yoghurt, mint, salt and garlic in a bowl and mix well to thin out the yoghurt a little. If the yoghurt is very thick, add up to 125 ml (½ cup) water to create a thinner sauce.

Drain the spaghetti and place in a large serving bowl. Pour the yoghurt sauce over the top and toss until the spaghetti strands are well coated with the sauce. Serve at room temperature with your choice of salad. It goes particularly well with cabbage salad with almonds (see page 91).

Kebab el karaz

SOUR CHERRY KEBAB BALLS

SERVES 4

500 g (1 lb 2 oz) minced (ground) lamb

1 small brown onion, finely chopped

1 red bird's eye chilli, finely chopped

1 teaspoon salt flakes

½ teaspoon freshly ground black pepper

2 tablespoons olive oil, plus extra for shaping

20 g (1½ tablespoons) butter

40 g (¼ cup) pine nuts

2 pieces Middle Eastern bread, cut into eighths, plus extra to serve

3 tablespoons roughly chopped flat-leaf parsley

SOUR CHERRY SAUCE

500 g (1 lb 2 oz) cherries, pitted and roughly chopped

2 tablespoons pomegranate molasses

juice of ½ lemon

2 teaspoons sugar

1 teaspoon ground cinnamon

This is a Syrian recipe from Aleppo, and what makes it truly Aleppan is the mix of hot and sweet flavours, which is typical of the cuisine. It's a style my mother uses when pickling and cooking some of her vegetarian dishes. Dried sour cherries can be hard to find, so here I've used fresh cherries and molasses instead. Alternatively, use drained, bottled morello cherries and halve the quantity of pomegranate molasses.

Place the lamb, onion, chilli, salt, pepper and 1 tablespoon olive oil in a bowl and mix together with your hands. Cover the bowl with cling film (plastic wrap) and refrigerate for about an hour.

Meanwhile, to make the cherry sauce, place all the ingredients and 250 ml (1 cup) water in a medium, heavy-based saucepan. Bring to the boil over high heat, then reduce the heat to low and simmer for 30–35 minutes, stirring every few minutes. Don't worry if the cherries break and fall apart – this will help to thicken the sauce.

Remove the lamb mixture from the fridge. Moisten your hands with a little olive oil to stop the mixture sticking to your fingers and form it into small meatballs (about 2 cm/¾ in in diameter).

Heat the remaining olive oil in a frying pan (skillet) over medium heat. Add the meatballs in batches, so as not to overcrowd the pan, and cook for 5 minutes or until nicely browned.

Add the meatballs to the cherry sauce and stir to coat well. Simmer gently for another 10–15 minutes.

Melt the butter in a small frying pan (skillet) over medium heat, add the pine nuts and fry until golden brown. Using a slotted spoon, remove about half the fried nuts and drain on kitchen paper (paper towels). Stir the remaining nuts and melted butter into the meatballs and cherry sauce.

Arrange the Middle Eastern bread pieces on a serving plate. Spoon the meatballs and sauce onto the bread and garnish with the parsley and remaining pine nuts.

Serve immediately with extra Middle Eastern bread and, if you like, some boiled rice or roasted potatoes and a dollop of natural yoghurt.

Shawarma & shanklish

SPICED BEEF STRIPS WITH AGED YOGHURT CHEESE

SERVES 6

---

1 teaspoon cumin seeds

1 teaspoon cloves

1 teaspoon black peppercorns

3 cardamom pods

1 teaspoon sweet paprika

½ teaspoon cayenne pepper

1½ teaspoons salt flakes

1 teaspoon ground pimento or seven-spice mix (see page 13)

1 kg (2¼ lb) beef rump or round steak, trimmed of fat and cut into thin strips

125 ml (½ cup) white wine vinegar

2 cloves garlic, crushed

2 brown onions, cut in half and thinly sliced

1 red (bell) pepper, seeds and membrane removed, cut in half and thinly sliced

180 ml (¾ cup) olive oil

3 pieces of Middle Eastern bread

1 × 200 g (7 oz) ball of mild shanklish

2 tomatoes, diced

small handful of mint

This is probably the most popular street food in Damascus. It is traditionally cooked the same way as a doner kebab. Layers of meat (normally beef or lamb) are placed on a large steel rod and cooked on a rotating plate against an open flame. Back in the day, the open flame was wood-fired, but these days it's a gas flame. In Syria, shawarma is traditionally served on a piece of Middle Eastern bread with hummus or tahini sauce (see pages 18 and 21), pickles, tomato, cucumber and onion.

Here is my recipe for a homestyle shawarma. The meat is softened with vinegar and seasoned with a beautiful array of spices, and I have added what I love best with cooked meat – cheese! Available from Middle Eastern grocers, shanklish is a lovely dried and slightly aged yoghurt cheese coated in dried oregano. If you're up for a challenge, try making it yourself (see page 47). Shanklish may be replaced with another crumbly cheese, such as a crumbly blue or vintage Cheddar.

The meat needs to marinate overnight so start this recipe a day ahead.

Using a mortar and pestle, crush the cumin seeds, cloves, peppercorns, cardamom pods, paprika, cayenne pepper, salt and pimento or seven-spice mix to a fine spice blend. Run the spice mix through a fine sieve and discard any large pieces or husks that cannot be crushed.

 Place the beef in a large bowl, add the spice blend, vinegar, garlic, onion, red (bell) pepper and 125 ml (½ cup) olive oil and mix until the beef is evenly coated. Cover and marinate in the fridge overnight to enhance the flavour and allow the vinegar to soften the meat.

 Heat the remaining olive oil in a large frying pan (skillet) over high heat. Drain the beef strips, then add to the pan and cook until nicely browned. If you cover the pan for a few minutes, the steam will speed up the cooking process without toughening or overcooking the beef.

 Arrange the Middle Eastern bread on a large serving platter and place the cooked beef in a mound in the middle. Crumble the shanklish cheese over the beef, followed by the diced tomato. Sprinkle the mint leaves over the top and serve immediately. If you like, serve with potato salad or cabbage salad with almonds (see pages 100 and 91).

Kafta wu batata bil saniyeh

ROASTED BEEF PATTIES & POTATOES

SERVES 6

———————————

70 g (¼ cup) tomato purée (paste)

1 teaspoon salt flakes

½ teaspoon freshly ground black pepper

1 teaspoon freshly grated nutmeg

1 teaspoon ground cinnamon

1 brown onion, thinly sliced

3 ripe tomatoes, thinly sliced

1 green (bell) pepper, seeds and membrane removed, thinly sliced

KAFTA PATTIES

300 g (11 oz) lean minced (ground) beef

1 small brown onion, grated

small handful of flat-leaf parsley, finely chopped

2 teaspoons seven-spice mix (see page 13)

2 teaspoons salt flakes

½ teaspoon freshly ground black pepper

2 tablespoons olive oil

POTATO LAYER

250 ml (1 cup) vegetable oil

3 maincrop or Russet potatoes, peeled and cut into 5 mm (¼ in) thick slices

———————————

My brother George and his wife Heather, absolutely adore this dish. Whenever they visit, Mum makes it for them on their first night here. It's a simple rustic dish that melts in your mouth. The layers of beef patties and potato are perfectly complemented by the light tomato sauce.

To make the kafta patties, place the meat, onion, parsley, seven-spice mix, salt and pepper in a bowl and knead until well combined. Lightly coat your hands lightly with olive oil, then form golf-ball-sized portions of the kafta mix into thin patties (you should have about 14–16 patties). Put the patties on a plate, then cover and refrigerate until needed.

For the potato layer, heat the vegetable oil in a shallow frying pan (skillet) over medium heat, add the potato slices in batches and cook until lightly golden on both sides. Remove and drain well on kitchen paper (paper towels).

Place the tomato purée (paste), salt, pepper, nutmeg, cinnamon and 300 ml (1¼ cups) warm water in a bowl and stir to combine.

Preheat the oven to 190°C (fan)/400°F/gas mark 6 and grease a deep 33 × 23 cm (13 x 9 in) baking dish or roasting pan.

Place a layer of patties on the base of the dish or pan and top with a layer of potatoes. Repeat with the remaining patties, and then the remaining potato slices. Scatter the onion slices over the potato, then the tomato and finally the green pepper. Pour the spiced tomato sauce evenly over the top, then cover with foil and bake for 1½–2 hours or until the potato slices have softened completely. Serve with a green salad, such as tabouli or fatoush (see pages 90 and 88).

Yakhnet iljej

SLOW-COOKED BROTH OF CHICKEN & CHICKPEAS

SERVES 6

250 g (1¼ cups) dried chickpeas

1 × 1.2–1.6 kg (2¾–3½ lb) chicken

2 bay leaves

1 teaspoon cloves

2 teaspoons salt flakes

400 g (2 cups) basmati rice

2 tablespoons olive oil

2 brown onions, roughly chopped

2 cloves garlic, crushed

30 g (2 tablespoons) butter

100 g (3½ oz) vermicelli noodles, broken into 2 cm (¾ in) lengths

½ teaspoon freshly grated nutmeg

1 teaspoon freshly ground black pepper

One night when I got home late from work I found a large Pyrex dish in the fridge (Pyrex has now taken over from Tupperware in Mum's kitchen!). Inside was a thick broth laced with shredded chicken, onion and beautiful large chickpeas. There was a container of rice as well. I really hit the jackpot with the leftovers that night, which were warm, filling and hearty. If you like, you could replace the chicken with cubed beef (topside works well here). Start this recipe the day before you need it.

Soak the chickpeas in a large bowl of water overnight. Rinse and drain. (If you are really pushed for time, omit this step and use two 400 g (14 oz) cans of chickpeas instead.)

Place the chicken in a large saucepan with the bay leaves, cloves and 1 teaspoon salt and cover completely with cold water. Bring to the boil, then reduce the heat and simmer over medium–low heat for 30–40 minutes or until the chicken is cooked through. Lift the chicken out of the stock and leave to cool for about 15 minutes. Remove the bay leaves and cloves from the stock. Strain the stock, discarding the solids, and reserve for later.

Meanwhile, if using dried chickpeas, bring a small saucepan of water to the boil, add the chickpeas and cook over high heat for 5–10 minutes. Reduce the heat to medium–low and cook for a further 30–40 minutes or until the chickpeas have softened. Drain the chickpeas and add them to the stock.

Remove the skin and bones from the chicken and shred the meat into large bite-sized pieces. Return to the stock.

Rinse the rice well, then soak in a bowl of warm water for about 30 minutes. Drain.

Meanwhile, heat the olive oil in a small frying pan (skillet) over medium heat, add the onion and garlic and cook until softened. Transfer this mixture to the stock, then cover and simmer gently over low heat for about 20 minutes.

Melt the butter in a medium saucepan over high heat, add the vermicelli and cook until golden brown, stirring constantly so they don't catch and burn. Add the drained rice and stir to coat well with the butter. Pour in 1 litre (4 cups) water, then season with the nutmeg, pepper and remaining salt and cook gently over low heat for 20–25 minutes until the rice has absorbed all the liquid, stirring every 5 minutes or so.

To serve, place a bed of rice in individual bowls and ladle over a generous amount of chicken, chickpeas and broth.

Betinjen maftouh

OPEN AUBERGINE

SERVES 4

---

250 g (9 oz) minced (ground) lamb

2 tablespoons olive oil

1 small onion, sliced

1 small maincrop or Russet potato,
peeled and diced

1 carrot, peeled and diced

1 small swede (rutabaga), peeled and diced

1 parsnip, peeled and diced

1 stick celery, diced

1 teaspoon ground cumin

1 teaspoon ground cinnamon

1 teaspoon sweet paprika

1 teaspoon freshly grated nutmeg

1 teaspoon salt flakes

1 × 420 g (15 oz) can crushed tomatoes

2 aubergines (eggplants)

natural yoghurt, to serve (optional)

I came up with this dish a couple of years ago when I took part in a food challenge. We were asked to create a recipe using the pre-packaged soup packs you buy in the supermarket, to which we were allowed to add a limited number of other ingredients. Much as I love soup, I had to be a little different. The result was a hearty Middle Eastern-influenced baked aubergine (eggplant) dish that leaves you feeling nourished and contented.

Cook the meat in a large non-stick frying pan (skillet) over medium-high heat until browned, breaking up any lumps with the back of a spoon. Remove the lamb with a slotted spoon and set aside, then drain the fat from the pan.

Heat the olive oil in the frying pan (skillet), add the onion, potato, carrot, swede (rutabaga), parsnip, celery, spices and salt and cook, stirring regularly, over medium heat for 15–20 minutes. Add the meat and crushed tomatoes and stir them in, then reduce the heat to low and simmer for about 10 minutes. Remove from the heat.

Preheat the oven to 190°C (fan)/400°F/gas mark 6.

Cut the aubergines (eggplants) in half lengthways, removing the green stalks. Using a small spoon or melon baller, scoop out most of the aubergine (eggplant) flesh, leaving a 5 mm–1 cm (¼–½ in) shell. Spoon the lamb and vegetable mix into the aubergine (eggplant) halves.

Place the aubergine (eggplant) halves on a non-stick baking tray (cookie sheet) and bake for 20–25 minutes. Leave to sit at room temperature for 5 minutes, then serve with a good dollop of yoghurt, if liked.

Macaroni bi haleeb

SPAGHETTI COOKED IN MILK

SERVES 4

---

300 g (11 oz) spaghetti

60 ml (¼ cup) olive oil

300 g (11 oz) skinless chicken breast fillet,
cut into thin strips

1 brown onion, finely chopped

1 clove garlic, crushed

2 teaspoons freshly grated nutmeg

1 teaspoon ground cinnamon

1 tablespoon salt flakes

½ teaspoon freshly ground black pepper

1 litre (4 cups) full-cream (whole) milk

1 tablespoon cornflour (cornstarch) mixed with
250 ml (1 cup) water

This is a beautiful dish my uncle's wife created for us when we visited them in Melbourne. I have never forgotten it. It's a simple warm recipe that reflects my beautiful Aunty Marta's love of nutmeg and cinnamon.

Cook the spaghetti in salted boiling water until al dente, following the packet instructions. Drain in a colander and rinse under cold water to stop the strands sticking together.

Meanwhile, heat 1 tablespoon olive oil in a medium frying pan (skillet) over high heat, add the chicken strips and cook for 5–8 minutes, tossing to seal. Set aside.

Preheat the oven to 190°C (fan)/400°F/gas mark 6.

Heat 1 tablespoon olive oil in a large saucepan over medium heat, add the onion and garlic and cook for about 5 minutes or until golden. Add the chicken, then the nutmeg, cinnamon, salt and pepper and stir to combine.

Increase the heat to high and pour in the milk. Cook, stirring, for about 7 minutes, then add the cornflour mixture and stir constantly to stop any lumps forming. When the mixture starts to thicken, reduce the heat to low and add the spaghetti to the pan. Simmer gently for about 5 minutes, stirring from time to time to stop it sticking to the pan.

Pour the mixture into a 30 × 18 × 6 cm (12 x 7 x 2½ in) non-stick baking dish and even out the surface with a spoon. Drizzle the remaining olive oil evenly over the top and bake for 20 minutes or until the top starts to turn golden brown. Remove from the oven and rest for about 10 minutes before serving. This is delicious with green beans in olive oil (see page 101) or aubergine (eggplant) salad (see page 96).

Riz bi fussool-ya

CANNELLINI BEAN, TOMATO & BEEF STEW

SERVES 4

---

500 g (1 lb 2 oz) rump, beef round or chuck steak, cut into 1–2 cm (½–¾ in) cubes

2 pieces of cassia bark or 1 cinnamon stick

2 bay leaves

3 teaspoons salt flakes

400 g (2 cups) dried cannellini or butter (lima) beans

60 g (4 tablespoons) butter

2 brown onions, roughly diced

4 cloves garlic, thinly sliced

2 × 420 g (15 oz) cans crushed or diced tomatoes

2 tablespoons tomato purée (paste)

½ teaspoon freshly ground black pepper

RICE WITH FRIED VERMICELLI

400 g (2 cups) basmati rice

2 tablespoons olive oil

100 g (3½ oz) vermicelli noodles, broken into 2 cm (¾ in) lengths

---

There are quite a few dishes across the Levant that combine beef with beans and rice, but this one is probably the most popular. It's amazing how much flavour you can get out of some pretty simple ingredients. This dish made a regular appearance on the dinner table while I was growing up. We would eat it with sides of fresh watercress, radish and my mother's beautiful homemade olives.

Place the beef, cassia or cinnamon, bay leaves and 2 teaspoons salt in a medium saucepan, cover with water and cook over medium–low heat for 50–55 minutes or until the beef is cooked. Remove the cassia or cinnamon and bay leaves from the pan.

Place the beans in a medium saucepan, cover with water and cook over medium heat for 30–35 minutes or until softened but still a little firm to the touch. If the water starts to boil over medium heat, reduce it to low. Drain and set aside.

Melt the butter in a medium frying pan (skillet), add the onion and garlic and cook over medium heat until lightly golden. Add this mixture to the beef, then stir in the beans, crushed tomatoes, tomato purée (paste), pepper and remaining salt and simmer for about 20 minutes.

Meanwhile, for the rice with fried vermicelli, rinse the rice and soak in a bowl of warm water for 20 minutes. Drain well. Heat the olive oil in a medium saucepan over medium heat and cook the vermicelli noodles for 4–5 minutes or until just brown, stirring constantly. Add the drained rice and stir to coat well in the oil, then pour in about 1 litre (4 cups) water and cook over low heat for 20–25 minutes or until the rice has absorbed all the liquid, stirring occasionally to stop it sticking to the pan.

Serve the beef and bean mixture on a bed of vermicelli rice.

Booza Abi

chocolata wu fistor halabeh

CHOCOLATE & PISTACHIO ICE-CREAM

SERVES 6

---

70 g (½ cup) raw pistachio nuts

200 g (1 cup) caster (superfine) sugar

8 egg yolks

1.2 litres (5 cups) double (heavy) cream

200 g (7 oz) cooking chocolate, broken into small pieces

1 vanilla pod (bean), sliced lengthways, seeds scraped

sesame and pistachio biscuits (cookies) (see page 169), to serve

---

When I first started to cook at home at the age of eight, it was mostly baked goods. Okay, I admit, it was mostly chocolate-flavoured baked goods. Pistachios were big in my family too – they could be found in my mother's fridge at all times and were eaten raw. In Arabic, pistachios are called 'fistor halabeh' which translates as 'the nut of Aleppo'. Syria is the second largest producer in the region and even has its own type of pistachio. It was inevitable that I would combine the two, and the result is this creamy ice-cream that isn't too sweet and has a little crunch.

Place the pistachio nuts in a food processor and process for about 2 minutes until finely chopped (don't overprocess or the nuts will become a paste). Tip into a small bowl and wipe out the processor bowl to clean it.

Process the sugar and egg yolks in a food processor until well combined. Set aside.

Place the cream, chocolate and vanilla seeds in a medium heavy-based saucepan over high heat and cook, stirring constantly, until the mixture is just below the boil and the chocolate has melted. Reduce the heat to low.

Pour the egg yolk mixture into the chocolate cream and stir until smooth and well combined. Cook, stirring, over low heat for 10–15 minutes or until the mixture has thickened enough to coat the back of a spoon. Fold in the chopped pistachios.

Pour the custard into a stainless-steel bowl or baking tray (cookie sheet) and let it cool at room temperature for about 30 minutes, then place in the fridge until it has cooled completely. This will take about 2–3 hours.

Take the chilled custard out of the fridge and churn it in an ice-cream maker, following the manufacturer's instructions. Place the ice-cream in the freezer for 3–4 hours or until firm.

If you don't have an ice-cream maker, transfer the cooled ice-cream mixture from the fridge to the freezer and leave it for 6–8 hours, stirring it with a wooden spoon every 1–2 hours for the first 4 hours, and then let it freeze firm without stirring.

Serve the ice-cream with the biscuits (cookies).

Booza bi maward

ROSEWATER ICE-CREAM

SERVES 6

---

200 g (1 cup) caster (superfine) sugar

8 egg yolks

1.2 litres (5 cups) double (heavy) cream

1 vanilla pod (bean), sliced lengthways, seeds scraped

60 ml (¼ cup) rosewater

¼ teaspoon rose-pink food colouring

100 g (⅔ cup) unsalted macadamias

When I first decided to put ice-cream on the menu at Almond Bar, one of the first flavours that sprang to mind was rosewater and the demand for it has been overwhelming. So much so, that when I took it off the menu during the colder months it was very quickly made clear to me that I had made a big mistake. It has been a permanent fixture on the menu ever since. This creamy piece of heaven is very simple to make and is beautiful on its own or with any dessert.

Process the sugar and egg yolks in a food processor until well combined. Set aside.

Place the cream and vanilla seeds in a medium heavy-based saucepan over medium heat and cook, stirring constantly, for 5–10 minutes or until the mixture is just below the boil. Remove from the heat and set aside for 5 minutes.

Pour the rosewater into the vanilla cream, then very gradually add the egg-yolk mixture, stirring constantly to prevent it from curdling, until smooth and well combined. Add the food colouring. Cook, stirring, over low heat for 10–15 minutes or until the colour is evenly mixed through and the custard has thickened enough to coat the back of a spoon.

Pour the custard into a stainless-steel bowl or baking tray (cookie sheet) and let it cool at room temperature for about 30 minutes, then place in the fridge until it has cooled completely. This will take about 2–3 hours.

Take the chilled custard out of the fridge and churn it in an ice-cream maker, following the manufacturer's instructions. Place the ice-cream in the freezer for 3–4 hours or until firm.

If you don't have an ice-cream maker, transfer the cooled ice-cream mixture from the fridge to the freezer and leave it for 6–8 hours, stirring it with a wooden spoon every 1–2 hours for the first 4 hours, and then let it freeze firm without stirring.

Shortly before you are ready to serve, pulse the macadamias in a food processor until roughly chopped. Scoop the ice-cream into bowls and sprinkle the macadamias over the top.

Shorebet tein

FIG SORBET

SERVES 6

---

6 dried figs, roughly chopped
125 ml (½ cup) boiling water
grated zest of 1 lemon
110 g (½ cup) caster (superfine) sugar
1 tablespoon liquid glucose
fresh fruit and double (heavy) cream, to serve

These days it is important to cater to people's different dietary requirements. It seemed unfair to offer our dairy eaters beautiful creamy ice-cream and not have something just as good for our non-dairy eaters. As a big fan of figs, I decided that dried figs would work best in this sticky sorbet.

Soak the chopped figs in the boiling water for about 15 minutes or until slightly softened.

Place the figs and their soaking water in a food processor, add the lemon zest and blend together until finely chopped, almost a smooth paste. Set aside.

Pour 500 ml (2 cups) water into a medium heavy-based saucepan. Add the sugar, glucose and fig paste and stir over medium heat until the sugar has dissolved. Reduce the heat to low and cook for a further 10 minutes.

Pour the fig mixture into a stainless-steel bowl or baking tray (cookie sheet) and let it cool at room temperature for about 30 minutes, then place in the fridge until it has cooled completely. This will take about 2–3 hours.

Take the chilled mixture out of the fridge and churn it in an ice-cream maker, following the manufacturer's instructions. Place the sorbet in the freezer for 3–4 hours or until firm.

If you don't have an ice-cream maker, transfer the cooled mixture from the fridge to the freezer and leave it for 6–8 hours, stirring it with a wooden spoon every 1–2 hours for the first 4 hours, and then let it freeze firm without stirring.

About 5 minutes before you're ready to serve, remove the sorbet from the freezer and let it soften slightly at room temperature. Serve with fresh seasonal fruit and a small dollop of cream.

Ghraybe

SEMOLINA SHORTBREAD

MAKES ABOUT 30 BISCUITS (COOKIES)

---

75 g (½ cup) self-raising (self-rising) flour

75 g (½ cup) plain (all-purpose) flour

180 g (1 cup) fine semolina flour

250 g (2 sticks) unsalted butter, cut into large cubes
and softened at room temperature

¾ teaspoon orange blossom water

150 g (⅔ cup) caster (superfine) sugar

30 blanched almonds

Ghraybe are butter biscuits (cookies) that are served with tea or coffee. I think of them as the shortbread of the Arab world. You can use this basic dough to make a whole variety of biscuits (cookies): top them with nuts, coat the dough balls with crushed pistachios, or make the balls larger and stuff them with dates or sugared, crushed walnuts. They are all wildly popular across Syria and Lebanon, and make wonderful gifts.

Sift the three flours together into a medium bowl and set aside.

In a separate bowl, beat the butter using a hand-held electric beater for 2 minutes or until light and fluffy. Sprinkle in the orange blossom water and sugar and beat for a further 3 minutes or until well combined. Add the flours and gently fold in with a metal spoon to form a dough. Cover and refrigerate for 15 minutes to give it a firmer texture.

Preheat the oven to 190°C (fan)/400°F/gas mark 6. Line two baking trays (cookie sheets) with baking paper.

Remove the dough from the fridge and shape it into 3 cm (1¼ in) balls. Place on the baking trays (cookie sheets) and press down lightly with the back of a soup spoon or dessertspoon to flatten each ball to a 1 cm (½ in) thick disc. Place an almond in the centre of each flattened dough ball and press down lightly to stop it falling off.

Bake for 25–30 minutes or until lightly golden. Cool on the trays (sheets) for a few minutes before transferring to a wire rack to cool for about 15 minutes. Serve with tea or coffee. Store in an airtight container for up to 2 weeks (if they last that long!).

Barazeh

SESAME & PISTACHIO BISCUITS

MAKES 25-30

---

150 g (1¼ sticks) unsalted butter, cut into large cubes and softened at room temperature

40 g (¼ cup) brown sugar

45 g (⅓ cup) icing (confectioners') sugar

1 teaspoon vanilla extract

1 egg

250 g (1⅔ cups) self-raising (self-rising) flour

70 g (½ cup) raw pistachio nuts, roughly chopped in a food processor

60 g (⅓ cup) sesame seeds

I have yet to meet anyone who comes back from Syria without a container of barazeh made in Damascus. I've even noticed the distinctive round containers popping up all over sweet (candy) shops and grocers in Sydney. The addictive flavour and satisfying crunch of these biscuits (cookies) make them hard to resist. I often have them for breakfast with my coffee – a perfect match. That said, they go just as well with a scoop (or two) of ice-cream.

Place the butter and sugars in a mixing bowl and beat with a hand-held electric beater until combined. Add the vanilla and egg and continue to beat until the butter becomes a little lighter and creamier – about 3–4 minutes. Sift in the flour then combine all the ingredients by hand to form a soft dough. Form into a ball, cover with cling film (plastic wrap) and rest in the fridge for about 30 minutes.

Preheat the oven to 190°C (fan)/400°F/gas mark 6. Line two baking trays (cookie sheets) with baking paper.

Remove the dough from the fridge and form into small balls (about 2–3 cm/¾–1¼ in). Flatten each one gently by hand to a 1 cm (½ in) thick disc.

Place the chopped pistachios on one plate and the sesame seeds on another. Press the bottom side of each biscuit (cookie) into the pistachios and the top side into the sesame seeds. Carefully shake off any excess nuts or seeds and place the biscuits (cookies) on the lined baking trays (cookie sheets). Leave about 5 cm (2 in) between each one to allow for spreading during cooking.

Bake for about 15 minutes until the biscuits (cookies) are golden brown. Cool on the trays for a few minutes before transferring to a wire rack for about 15 minutes. Serve with tea or coffee. Store in an airtight container for up to 2 weeks.

Namoura

SWEET SEMOLINA & COCONUT SLICE

MAKES ABOUT 30 PIECES

550 g (2½ cups) fine semolina

100 g (1¼ cups) desiccated
(dry unsweetened) coconut

220 g (1 cup) sugar

125 g (1 stick) unsalted butter, melted

280 g (1 cup) natural yoghurt

2 teaspoons baking powder

2 tablespoons tahini

50 g (⅓ cup) blanched almonds, halved lengthways
(you can buy them like this)

ORANGE BLOSSOM SYRUP

440 g (2 cups) sugar

juice of 1 lemon

2 tablespoons orange blossom water

When deciding on the restaurant menu, I generally take a few factors into account: the season, customer feedback, friends and family, availability of ingredients, and my sister Carol. When we put this slice on our dessert menu, I realised why Carol agreed to it – she ate more of it than anyone else! This sticky slice of coconut heaven is popular all over the Middle East: some people leave the coconut out (I think they're borderline crazy!), while others top it with walnuts or pistachios instead of almonds. This is the way I like it.

Mix together the semolina, coconut, sugar, butter, yoghurt and baking powder in a bowl to form a smooth batter. Cover it with cling film (plastic wrap) and let it rest for 6 hours at room temperature.

Preheat the oven to 190°C (fan)/400°F/gas mark 6.

Grease a 28 × 18 × 5 cm (11 x 7 x 2 in) baking pan by rubbing the tahini all over the base and side with the tips of your fingers.

Pour the batter into the pan and spread it out evenly. Score 5 cm (2 in) squares on the surface and place half an almond in the centre of each square. Bake for about 40 minutes or until the surface is golden and crisp.

Meanwhile, to prepare the syrup, place the sugar and 250 ml (1 cup) water in a small saucepan and boil over high heat until it reaches a thick syrup consistency (about 5 minutes). Add the lemon juice and orange blossom water, then remove from the heat and let it cool for 15–20 minutes.

Take the slice out of the oven and pour the syrup evenly over the top. The hot slice will soak it all up. Leave it to cool for 15 minutes, then cut into squares following the scored lines.

Namoura will keep for up to 10 days in an airtight container. It is best stored in the fridge, but take it out a few minutes before you want to eat it to let it soften.

Sfouf

TURMERIC CAKE

SERVES 6

---

440 g (2 cups) fine semolina

160 g (1 cup) plain (all-purpose) flour

¼ teaspoon ground turmeric

1 teaspoon baking powder

250 g (2 sticks) butter, melted and cooled for 10–15 minutes

385 g (1¾ cups) sugar

375 ml (1½ cups) milk

1½ tablespoons tahini

70 g (½ cup) flaked (slivered) almonds

I only ever saw this cake in the Middle Eastern sweet (candy) shops when I was growing up – it wasn't one Mum made at home. Not understanding what turmeric was, I often wondered how the cake could be so yellow. Eventually I figured it out and decided to try cooking it myself. The colour and flavour make this cake a stand-out.

Preheat the oven to 190°C (fan)/400°F/gas mark 6.

Place the semolina, flour, turmeric and baking powder in a large bowl and stir to combine.

In a separate bowl, combine the butter, sugar, milk and 60 ml (¼ cup) water. Pour into the dry ingredients and stir to make a batter.

Grease a deep 23 cm (9 in) round cake pan by rubbing the tahini all over the base and side with the tips of your fingers.

Pour the cake batter into the tin and sprinkle with the flaked (slivered) almonds. Bake for 35–40 minutes or until browned on top. Remove from the oven and cool in the pan for a few minutes, then turn out onto a wire rack to cool completely. Serve with tea or coffee. Store in an airtight container for a week.

Ashta

MIDDLE EASTERN CLOTTED CREAM

MAKES ABOUT 250 G (1 CUP)

———————————

1.2 litres (5 cups) milk
45 ml (3 tablespoons) freshly squeezed lemon juice
(from about 2 lemons)

———————————

There are tons of recipes for ashta. Some include orange blossom water and white bread, others call for the addition of ricotta cheese. This is the most traditional way to make it.

Place the milk in a medium heavy-based saucepan and stir over high heat just until it is just below the boil. Reduce the heat to low and simmer gently. Pour in the lemon juice and stir the mixture slowly as the milk separates. After 3–4 minutes you will notice that curds start to form around the edge of the pan.

Remove from the heat and pour through a fine sieve that has been lined with kitchen paper (paper towels). Leave the ashta to drain and cool for about an hour at room temperature, then refrigerate for at least 2–3 hours to develop a thicker texture.

This can be enjoyed in so many ways, but the simplest way to serve it is with fresh fruit.

Atayef

DEEP-FRIED PANCAKES WITH CLOTTED CREAM

SERVES 6–8

---

500 g (2 cups) ashta (Middle Eastern clotted cream; see page 174)

1 litre (4 cups) vegetable oil

about 500 ml (2 cups) ater (sugar syrup; see page 7), or to taste

50 g (⅓ cup) raw pistachio nuts, crushed

PANCAKES

300 g (2 cups) plain (all-purpose) flour

2½ teaspoons baking powder

¼ teaspoon dried yeast dissolved in 2 tablespoons warm water

2 teaspoons sugar

I absolutely adore this dessert. It is worth every calorie! It has everything you want in a dessert – a smooth creaminess that is not too heavy, a bit of crunch and the option to sweeten it as much as you want.

Start by making the batter for the pancakes. Combine the flour, baking powder, dissolved yeast mixture, sugar and 625 ml (2½ cups) water in a bowl and mix together with a whisk or hand-held electric beater until smooth and lump-free. You may want to transfer the batter to a pouring jug (pitcher) or have a ladle handy for easy pouring. Cover and rest at room temperature for 1 hour.

Heat a medium non-stick frying pan (skillet) over medium heat. Once hot, pour in enough batter to make pancakes about 8 cm (3¼ in) in diameter. Cook for 1–1½ minutes until all the bubbles that form on the surface have burst and the uncooked batter is no longer shiny. The underside should be nicely golden but not burnt. You only want to cook the pancakes on one side, so as soon as they are ready, remove them from the pan and let them cool on a plate. Repeat with the remaining batter to make about 12 pancakes.

Scoop out just over a tablespoon of clotted cream and spread it evenly over the uncooked side of a pancake, leaving a 1 cm (½ in) border around the edge. Fold the pancake in half to create a semi-circle and press the edges together. From this you will know whether to adjust the amount of clotted cream – it should not ooze through the pancake or feel skimpy. Repeat with the remaining pancakes and cream, then place them on a tray, cover with cling film (plastic wrap) and refrigerate for about an hour.

Heat the oil in a large saucepan over high heat for about 8 minutes. Gently lower a couple of cream-filled pancakes into the oil and cook until they are crisp and golden on both sides. Remove from the oil with a slotted spoon or tongs and drain on kitchen paper (paper towels). Repeat with the remaining pancakes.

Arrange all the cooked pancakes on a plate, drizzle the sugar syrup liberally over the top and finish with the crushed pistachios.

Note
Traditionally, the cooked pancakes are taken from the oil and put straight into a bowl of sugar syrup. You can do this too, if you want a sweeter finish.

Chocolata

SHREDDED PASTRY WITH CHOCOLATE CREAM

MAKES 10

———————————

300 g (11 oz) kataifi pastry

50 g (¼ cup) butter, melted

80 g (½ cup) hazelnuts, crushed

150 ml (⅔ cup) ater (sugar syrup; see page 7)

CHOCOLATE CREAM

600 ml (2½ cups) double (heavy) cream

250 ml (1 cup) milk

250 g (9 oz) milk cooking chocolate, broken into pieces

2 tablespoons orange blossom water

50 g (⅓ cup) cornflour (cornstarch) blended with 60 ml (¼ cup) milk to make a paste

———————————

Traditionally, chocolate doesn't feature much in Middle Eastern desserts, but the demand for chocolate in the restaurant got the better of me. It didn't take much to twist my arm, and I came up with the following dish. Kataifi is a finely shredded pastry that looks similar to vermicelli noodles, but has a beautiful crunchy texture when cooked.

Start by making the chocolate cream. Place the cream and milk in a medium heavy-based saucepan over medium heat and bring to just below the boil. Add the chocolate and stir constantly until melted. Add the orange blossom water, then the cornflour (cornstarch) paste and whisk vigorously to stop any lumps forming. (If you do not have a steel whisk, use a wooden spoon, but reduce the heat to low.) When the cream has thickened to the consistency of pouring custard, remove the pan from the heat and set aside to cool at room temperature. Refrigerate for at least 4 hours to allow the chocolate cream to thicken and cool completely.

Preheat the oven to 190°C (fan)/400°F/gas mark 6. Line a baking tray (cookie sheet) with baking paper.

Pull the kataifi apart by hand to make it workable. Ensure you are in a cool space, without any breeze to dry out the pastry. Pull off a small handful of the pastry and loosely work it between your palms to the size of a tennis ball. Place the ball on the baking tray (cookie sheet) and gently press down to flatten it into a disc shape. Repeat with the remaining pastry to make 20 discs.

Using a pastry brush, lightly brush the discs with melted butter, then place in the oven and bake for 20–25 minutes or until golden. Remove from the oven and allow to cool completely.

For each serving, place a kataifi disc on a serving plate and top with 2 tablespoons of the chocolate cream. Spread the cream out evenly, then gently place another disc on top. Sprinkle lightly with the crushed hazelnuts and serve with sugar syrup on the side so everyone can help themselves.

kataifi

Znood il seit

LADY'S ARMS

SERVES 6

---

1 tablespoon plain (all-purpose) flour

1 × 375 g (13 oz) packet filo (phyllo) pastry

80 g (⅓ cup) butter, melted

400–500 g (1¾–2 cups) ashta (Middle Eastern clotted cream; see page 174), plus extra to serve (optional)

1 egg, lightly beaten

1 kg (2¼ lb) ghee or clarified butter

150 ml (⅔ cup) ater (sugar syrup; see page 7), plus extra to serve

strawberries, to serve (optional)

A known fact . . . if you take these to a dinner party or barbecue, you will be by far the most celebrated guest! Many people ask me what they should buy when they visit a Middle Eastern sweet (candy) shop. These crisp golden logs are always the first thing I suggest. They are absolutely exquisite – light and fluffy and not too difficult to prepare. If you prefer, you could use 1 litre (4 cups) of vegetable oil instead of the clarified butter.

Sprinkle the flour over a clean, dry bench, then place the filo (phyllo) sheets on the bench. Using kitchen scissors, cut half the sheets into 8 cm (3¼ in) wide strips and stack together. Cut the remaining filo (phyllo) sheets into 7 cm (2¾ in) wide strips and stack together. Discard any excess pastry. Have a slightly damp cloth or tea (dish) towel handy to cover the unused filo (phyllo) sheets while you work, to prevent them from drying out.

Take three of the 8 cm (3¼ in) strips and place on the bench, lightly brushing between the layers with butter. Do not brush the surface of the top strip. Place just over a tablespoon of clotted cream on the bottom end of the pastry, leaving a 1 cm (½ in) gap on both edges. Fold the sides of the pastry over the cream, making sure they are completely covering the sides of the cream, then roll up the pastry to form a neat log, enclosing the filling.

Next, take three of the 7 cm (2¾ in) strips and brush lightly with butter between the layers. This time you need to brush the surface of the top strip as well. Place the log at the bottom end of the pastry and roll it up like a cigar. Dip your finger in the beaten egg and smooth it over the seam to stop the pastry opening during cooking. Place on a tray lined with baking paper, seam-side down. Repeat with the remaining pastry and filling to make about 12–14 lady's arms, then refrigerate for an hour.

Melt the ghee or clarified butter in a large heavy-based saucepan over high heat and heat for about 4 minutes. Working in small batches so you don't overcrowd the pan, gently lower a few lady's arms into the butter and cook until they are golden brown all over and the pastry is crisp. Remove with a slotted spoon and drain on kitchen paper (paper towels) for about 2 minutes. Drizzle with the sugar syrup and serve immediately.

Traditionally lady's arms are served with an additional bowl of Middle Eastern clotted cream and extra sugar syrup. And I think they go perfectly with fresh strawberries.

Ward et shem

ROSE OF DAMASCUS

MAKES ABOUT 25

————————

1 tablespoon plain (all-purpose) flour

1 × 375 g (13 oz) packet filo (phyllo) pastry

125 g (1 stick) unsalted butter, melted

350 g (1½ cups) ashta (Middle Eastern clotted cream; see page 174)

100 g (¼ cup) orange blossom jam (or another jam if you prefer)

70 g (½ cup) raw pistachio nuts, crushed

100 ml (½ cup) ater (sugar syrup; see page 7)

————————

The actual Rose of Damascus has a beautiful scent unlike that of any other rose, and this cherished dessert is so named because of its resemblance to the fabled rose. The first time I tried it was in Syria when I was a child. A guest had made a tray of these for my grandmother to thank her for a dinner invitation. Twenty years later, I still remember every detail of the colour, texture and creaminess of the dessert. What a way to say thank you!

Preheat the oven to 180°C (fan)/400°F/gas mark 6.

Sprinkle the flour over a clean, dry bench, then flatten out the filo (phyllo) pastry sheets on the bench. Using a 5–6 cm (2–2½ in) round cutter, cut out about 25 rounds from the pastry stack.

Place the rounds in a large deep baking tray (cookie sheet) (or two smaller ones) and pour the melted butter over the top so they are generously covered.

Bake for about 20 minutes or until the pastry is just starting to turn golden. Remove and leave to cool for about 10 minutes, then transfer the rounds to a serving plate.

Split each round horizontally into three layers. Place a generous teaspoon of clotted cream on the bottom layer, then add a second pastry layer and top this with another teaspoon of cream. Finish with the final layer of pastry, then decorate with a small teaspoon of orange blossom jam and a sprinkling of crushed pistachios. Drizzle a little sugar syrup over each one and serve.

Mafroukeh

SEMOLINA FUDGE

SERVES 4–6

---

220 g (1 cup) fine semolina

180 g (¾ cup) ghee or unsalted butter, cut into cubes

220 g (1 cup) sugar

1 tablespoon rosewater

170 g (¾ cup) ashta (Middle Eastern clotted cream;
see page 174)

40 g (¼ cup) blanched almonds, roasted
and roughly chopped

40 g (¼ cup) pine nuts, roasted

35 g (¼ cup) raw pistachio nuts, ground

80 g (¼ cup) orange blossom jam
or your favourite jam

When I was a child, I often saw this intriguing dessert on my aunty's table. I wondered what it was, but was a bit too cautious to try it. I came across it again as a teenager in a sweet (candy) shop and my curiosity got the better of me. This time I tasted it, and of course it was absolutely delicious!

Place the semolina in a medium saucepan and toast over high heat for a couple of minutes, stirring constantly. Reduce the heat to medium, add the ghee or butter and stir until it has melted completely. Add 500 ml (2 cups) hot water, increase the heat to high and cook, stirring, until well combined and thickened slightly.

Reduce the heat to medium, add the sugar and rosewater and stir until the sugar has dissolved completely. This should take about 6–7 minutes, and in the process the fudge mixture will thicken to dough-like consistency.

To serve, spread the warm fudge over a serving plate, spread the clotted cream over it and sprinkle with the almonds, pine nuts and pistachios. Finish with small dollops of jam and serve.

Raha bi fest

TURKISH DELIGHT WITH PISTACHIO

SERVES 6

---

42 g (¼ cup) powdered gelatine

660 g (3 cups) sugar

60 ml (¼ cup) orange blossom water

100 g (⅔ cup) raw pistachio nuts (or any nut you like)

80 g (1 cup) desiccated (dry unsweetened) coconut

People absolutely love Turkish delight, and even though I have a sweet tooth myself, I sometimes find it a bit too sticky for my liking. Here is the homemade Salloum version, which hits the spot perfectly. When we were kids, my mother used to make this coconut-covered, pistachio-laden version every Easter and Christmas to serve to people visiting during the festivities.

In a small bowl, mix together the gelatine and 60 ml (¼ cup) water until dissolved. Set aside.

Pour 250 ml (1 cup) water into a medium saucepan and bring to the boil over high heat. Add the sugar and stir until dissolved, then add the gelatine mixture and orange blossom water and mix well to combine.

When the mixture comes to the boil, reduce the heat and simmer for about 20 minutes, stirring every couple of minutes so the mixture doesn't stick to the bottom of the pan. Just before the cooking time is up, stir in the nuts, then remove the pan from the heat.

Carefully pour the mixture into a medium (about 15 cm/6 in) non-stick tart or pie tin. Leave to cool for a couple of hours, then cover with cling film (plastic wrap) and leave to set for at least 8 hours at room temperature.

To remove the raha from the tin, pour some warm water into a large bowl and slowly lower the tin into the water (being careful not to get any water in the tin). The raha will start to loosen from the side.

Turn out the raha onto a large chopping board then, using a sharp knife, cut it evenly into square or diamond-shaped portions.

Place the coconut in a medium bowl, then add a few pieces of raha at a time and toss to coat in the coconut. Serve with the pistachio side facing up. These will keep for about a week in an airtight container (don't store them in the fridge or they will harden, making them less pleasant to eat).

-or halabeh

Halawet

SWEETENED CHEESE

SERVES 6

---

500 g (1 lb 2 oz) 'sweet cheese' or fresh mozzarella

330 g (1½ cups) sugar

440 g (2 cups) fine semolina

1 tablespoon orange blossom water

120 ml (½ cup) ater (sugar syrup; see page 7), plus extra to serve (optional)

ashta (Middle Eastern clotted cream; see page 174) and crushed pistachios, to serve

---

My godmother Nadia is an absolute genius at making this dessert. It takes a lot of strength and persistence to get it right, and she puts in a huge amount of time and love. It is traditionally made with Akawi cheese, but it is quite salty, so it's best to use mozzarella or, if possible, buy the specific 'sweet cheese' in Middle Eastern grocers. This sweet is made all over the Levant region, with slight differences in the amount of sugar and semolina added. Some recipes omit the orange blossom water or replace it with rosewater.

Thickly slice the cheese. If you are using mozzarella, soak it in cold water for about 2 hours to remove some of the saltiness. If you are using sweet cheese there is no need to soak it.

Bring 875 ml (3½ cups) water to the boil in a medium saucepan over high heat. Add the sugar and stir until dissolved. Reduce the heat to medium and pour in the semolina and orange blossom water. Mix well to combine.

If using mozzarella, drain it well. Add a few slices of cheese at a time to the semolina mixture, stirring constantly so the cheese melts evenly into the liquid before adding the next batch. Once all the cheese has melted and the mixture starts to come away from the side of the pan, remove the pan from the heat. If you find the cheese is a little slow to melt, increase the heat to high for a minute or two while you stir the mixture together.

Pour half the sugar syrup onto a clean, dry surface and spread it out evenly. Turn out the warm cheese mixture onto the syrup and smooth the surface as thinly as possible (about 4–5 mm/¼ in thick is ideal) with the back of a wooden spoon to create a sheet of sweetened cheese. This may take a little while. Pour on the remaining syrup and spread it over the cheese with your fingers.

Leave the mixture for about 30 minutes until it is set and cool enough to touch. Cut the sweetened cheese into 5 cm (2 in) wide strips and serve with a spoonful of clotted cream, a drizzle of extra syrup (if you like it really sweet) and a sprinkling of crushed pistachios.

il jiben

Riz bi haleeb

MILK & RICE PUDDING

SERVES 6–8

1.75 litres (7¼ cups) milk

60 ml (¼ cup) rosewater

165 g (¾ cup) sugar

220 g (1 cup) short-grain or medium-grain rice

crushed walnuts and jam, to serve (optional)

My brother Steven absolutely loves this dessert, and so do I. It is very popular at the restaurant too – I guess everyone enjoys a little rice pudding. The really special element in this recipe is the subtle flavour of rosewater. While it's normally served chilled, you could also eat it warm.

Place the milk, rosewater and sugar in a large saucepan and bring to the boil over medium–high heat, stirring to prevent the milk solids from sticking to the bottom.

Stir in the rice, then reduce the heat to low and cook, stirring occasionally, for 40–50 minutes or until the rice is cooked and the mixture has thickened slightly, although it will still be quite wet at this stage.

Remove from the heat and cool to room temperature, then refrigerate for 3 hours or until chilled. If you like, serve with crushed walnuts and a dollop of your favourite jam on top.

Semes–me–yeh

ROASTED PEANUT & SESAME SEED DIAMONDS

MAKES ABOUT 30 PIECES

---

500 g (3⅓ cups) roasted unsalted peanuts (skins removed)

500 g (3⅓ cups) sesame seeds

375 g (1 cup) honey

2 tablespoons tahini

For as long as I can recall, my Aunt Azizi has arrived at family gatherings with a plate of these. She wouldn't dare forget, knowing how much my father and sister love them! Even now, when I see those thin sesame bars in the supermarket, I think of my aunt and how beautifully she makes these. I may be biased, but I think her sesame diamonds are far more special than the bought version – and so easy to make.

Preheat the oven to 200°C (fan)/425°F/gas mark 7.

Crush the peanuts by pulsing them in a food processor about three times so that they are still quite chunky. Set aside.

Spread out the sesame seeds on a baking tray (cookie sheet) and toast in the oven for about 20 minutes, stirring every 5 minutes so the seeds around the edge of the tray (sheet) don't burn. They should be nicely golden but not too dark. Remove from the oven.

Heat the honey in a medium–large saucepan over medium heat for about 5 minutes, then reduce the heat to low and simmer for a further 15 minutes.

Add the sesame seeds and peanuts to the honey and mix well. Turn off the heat.

Grease a round pie plate or medium baking tray (cookie sheet) by rubbing the tahini all over the base and sides with the tips of your fingers. Pour in the nut and sesame mixture and spread it out evenly, pressing gently to smooth the surface. Let it sit for 5 minutes, then, while the mixture is still warm, score diamond shapes on the top – I usually make the diagonal lines about 2 cm (¾ in) apart. Leave to set for 10 minutes or so, then turn out the bars onto a clean, dry bench.

Store the diamonds in an airtight container at room temperature away from direct sunlight. They should last for about a week.

Kanefi bi

MIDDLE EASTERN CLOTTED CREAM WITH GOLDEN BREADCRUMBS

SERVES 6

---

600 ml (2½ cups) milk

300 ml (1¼ cups) double (heavy) cream

50 g (⅓ cup) cornflour (cornstarch)

60 ml (¼ cup) orange blossom water

150 g (1½ cups) dried breadcrumbs

ater (sugar syrup; see page 7), for drizzling

raw pistachio nuts, to serve (optional)

My Aunt Adel makes the most amazing kanefi, and never comes to a family gathering without it. In other parts of the Middle East, a range of nuts replace the creamy filling. There is no sugar in this recipe, but you can add as much or as little sugar syrup as you like.

Whisk together the milk, cream and cornflour (cornstarch) in a medium bowl until well combined. Set aside.

Pour the orange blossom water into a medium saucepan and simmer for about 2 minutes. Add the cream mixture and cook over medium heat, stirring constantly to ensure it doesn't stick to the bottom of the pan. Once the mixture starts to thicken to the consistency of custard, remove it from the heat and set aside to cool slightly.

Place the breadcrumbs in a dry frying pan (skillet) and cook over medium–high heat, stirring to make sure the crumbs brown lightly and evenly. (Alternatively, toast the crumbs in a preheated 200°C (fan)/425°F/gas mark 7 oven for 15–20 minutes, tossing twice during this time.) Allow the crumbs to cool completely.

Spread half the crumbs over the base of a medium non-stick baking tray (about 18 × 15 cm/7 x 6 in). Pour the cream mixture over the crumbs, then finish with an even scattering of the remaining breadcrumbs. Leave to set for about an hour. While still warm, spoon into bowls and serve with a jug (pitcher) of sugar syrup for everyone to help themselves. Garnish with a sprinkling of pistachios, if liked.

ashta

ACKNOWLEDGEMENTS

Being from an average Arab family with 16 aunties and uncles, there are just a few people I would like to thank for getting me to this point in my life and of course to this little book here . . .

To my mother and father, Violet and Michael Salloum, you have made my brothers, sister and me the people we are today. You have only ever lifted us up to the highest points, always supporting us through every step. You have constantly given to us even when you struggled. I will forever be grateful for being so blessed with such amazing guides in my life. Mum, thanks for letting me steal some of your recipes and make unorthodox changes to them. Dad, thanks for always trying to feed us. Oh and thanks for the nose!

To my incredible sister, mentor in life, best buddy and laughing partner, Carol. You started this journey for me. Without your dreams and perseverance, I wouldn't be here. Your soothing words and love (and occasional knife throwing!) have always pushed me to get through the toughest of times. There simply aren't the words to express what you have brought to my life.

Michelle Gomes, your support and encouragement during the writing of this book have been constant and untiring. You knew exactly how I wanted to pour my heart out onto a page.

To Megan Dunn, for answering all my silly cooking questions and listening to my 187 worries from time to time. You're the best, Megs!

To my cousin, Rima Hanna, your strength and love, respect and wisdom have made my world a better place. You taught me to fall in love with this great cuisine all over again.

My aunties, Azizi and Adele, and my godmother, Nadia, for letting me annoy you with questions about the food you cook so beautifully. Thank you to George and Adel Jarouge, for taking the time to make real shanklish for this book. What an amazing process to watch . . . a bit of Zwaitini in Sydney!

To my brothers, George and Steven, and their wives, Heather and Tatiana, your love, support and encouragement has been unsurpassed in every way. (Steven, people will not ask you for your autograph because your name is in the book!)

Fiorella Amarino, my adopted nonna, thank you for teaching me that there is no room in the world for stupid people!

Carol and I have the utmost appreciation and love for our staff at Almond Bar, past and present. Thank you to Shmitty (Tony Jarouge), Edward Charles, Islam Sahidul, Sunil Shrestha, Le Tran, Ben, Alex (li'l friend), Nancy, Kelly and Katie. You guys are da bomb (insert bomb sound here)!

Thank you to Maeve O'Mara, for convincing me to run one of her food tours and allowing me to educate so many people about the astonishing food of the Middle East. Also to Suzy Brien, for keeping me organised.

Christine Manfield, you are a true inspiration to so many female chefs, and you don't even have to try.

Katy Holder, I appreciate your honest feedback and guidance when testing my recipes – you're a gem. Thank you to all those who participated in recipe testing and for dealing with my many questions or confusing instructions.

To the people who found me in the tiny room called Almond Bar . . . At Penguin, Julie Gibbs, you are one incredible and talented publisher. Thank you for giving me the opportunity of a lifetime. To my most fabulous editor, Rachel Carter, every email made me smile or laugh, even when you were asking about my grey hairs! You are unbelievably kind-hearted and so damn patient! Nicole Abadee, thank you for polishing my recipe introductions so beautifully. Your encouragement makes a person feel all warm inside. Katrina O'Brien, thank you for your support. Emily O'Neill, you have made this book look amazing – the colours and pages are a dancing wonderland in my heart. Megan Pigott, don't use my eyebrow joke! You are the coolest shoot producer around, and one hell of an organiser too. Rob Palmer, love your work, you are one ridiculously awesome (and funny) photographer – S Dawg. Matt Page, stylist extraordinaire, the ashta photo says it all. Thank you for making my food of the earth look like food of the kings.

Finally, to my beautiful Teta Melia. Thank you for passing on your love of real Syrian food to your daughter, Violet. I hope we will meet again in Syria soon. ◆

INDEX

*The publisher would like to thank
Rosemary Cole and Ursula Burgoyne
for their ceramics.*

First published in the UK in 2014 by:
Jacqui Small LLP
74–77 White Lion Street
London N1 9PF

First published by Penguin Group (Australia), 2013

10 9 8 7 6 5 4 3 2 1

Design and illustration by Emily O'Neill © Penguin Group (Australia)

Photography by Rob Palmer

Styling by Matt Page

Typeset in Calluna by Post Pre-press Group, Brisbane, Queensland

Colour separation by Splitting Image Colour Studio, Clayton, Victoria

Printed and bound in China by 1010 Printing International Ltd

A catalogue record of this book is avaialable from the British Library

ISBN: 978-1-909342-57-6

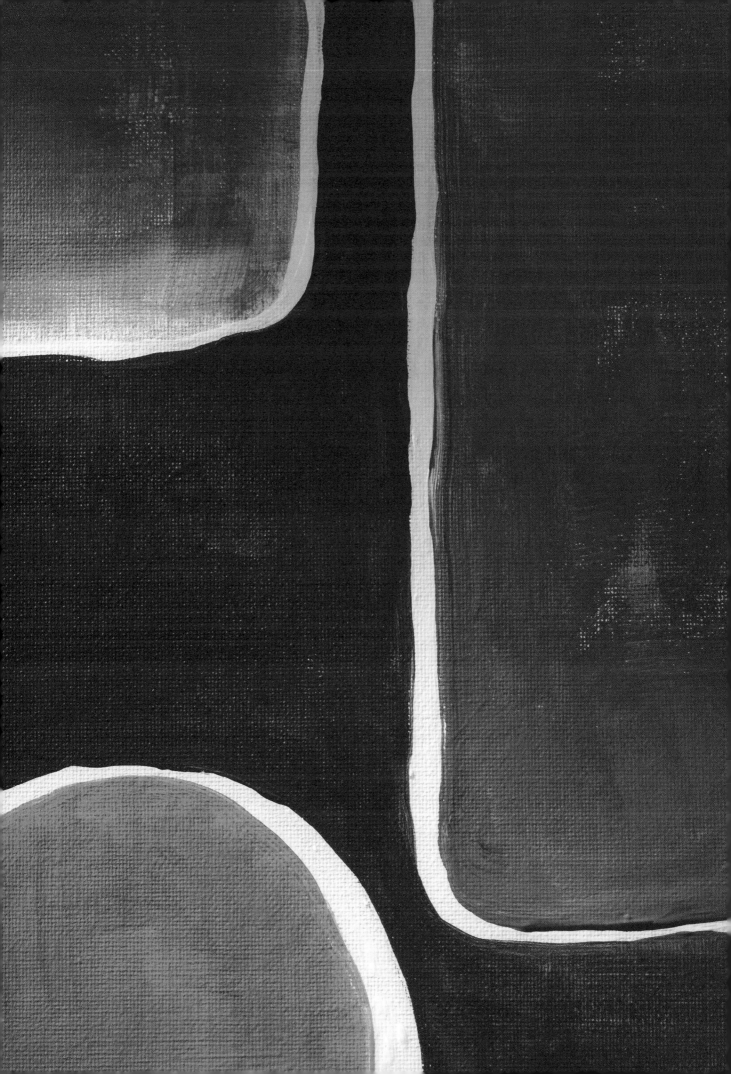